MASTERING YOUR INNER GAME

Stories of Overcoming Mountains with Mindset

JENN SCALIA - AJ MIHRZAD
JONO PETROHILOS – CAT ALMANZOR
MARY ALLISON BROWN - VITALE BUFORD
SHAWN HENSON - SUSANNA ESTHER KASHIEMER
SARA KIRSCH – CHRISTY LITTLE
ROSEANNEY LIU – JEN RYAN
ROSITA SZATKOWSKA - SALLY THURLEY

MASTERING YOUR INNER GAME

COPYRIGHT 2018 AJ MIHRZAD, JENN SCALIA

This work is licensed under a Creative Commons Attribution-Noncommercial-No Derivative Works 4.0 International License.

Attribution — You must attribute the work in the manner specified by the author or licensor (but not in any way that suggests that they endorse you or your use of the work).

Noncommercial — You may not use this work for commercial purposes.

No Derivative Works — You may not alter, transform, or build upon this work.

Inquiries about additional permissions should be directed to: jennebom@gmail.com

The sole purpose of this book is to educate and inspire. There is no guarantee made by the authors or the publisher that anyone following the ideas, tips, suggestions, techniques, or strategies will become successful. The author and publisher shall have neither liability nor responsibility to anyone with respect to any loss or damage caused, or alleged to be caused, directly or indirectly by the information contained in this book.

PRINT ISBN 978-1-7270-7097-2

CONTENTS

AJ MIHRZAD—From My Worst Point in Life to a Million-Dollar Business 5

JENN SCALIA—From Corporate Captive to Motivated Maven 19

JONO PETROHILOS—Failure is Not the Opposite of Success... It's Part of the Process 27

CAT ALMANZOR—Fearless Faith: Transforming Pain into Power 37

MARY ALLISON BROWN—From Unsustainable to Unboxed: Releasing the Weight of Limiting Beliefs to Thrive 45

VITALE BUFORD—Let Fear Be Your Compass 53

SHAWN HENSON—The Next Right Step 61

SUSANNA ESTHER KASHIEMER—The Power of Perspective . 71

SARA KIRSCH—When Life Gives You Lemons, Add Limes and Make Margaritas! 84

CHRISTY LITTLE—A Dreamer, A Believer, and an Achiever in Transformation 96

MASTERING YOUR INNER GAME

ROSEANNEY LIU—I Am In Control Over Myself 103

JEN RYAN—Take Your Power Back for Success 112

ROSITA SZATKOWSKA—From Homeless to Corporate 120

SALLY THURLEY—We Are All The Cosmic Dancer 129

From My Worst Point in Life to a Million-Dollar Business

Lessons from hitting rock-bottom

AJ MIHRZAD

I WANT TO SHARE with you something I've never talked about openly. It was actually the worst experience of my entire life, and it happened recently. I'm getting emotional as I think about it, because it's really difficult to share with you everything I went through.

You see, when I first started my online business, I struggled terribly. I really didn't know what I was doing. I was trying to get clients online and was having a hard time selling my services. I didn't quite understand how to deliver results. You know, I'm a bit of a technical dunce, so, when it comes to using computers and the Internet, I'm not the sharpest tool in the box.

So, as I was struggling to build my business, I had a lot of mental resistance, which was exacerbated by negative thoughts; also, financially, I was not doing very well. It was extremely difficult for me to transition from personal training to being a full-time online coach.

I remember this one day like it was yesterday. It was a Tuesday night, and as I was pulling up to my driveway alongside my house, the first thing I noticed was my lights were on. I remember saying to myself, "Whoa! Why are my lights on?" I always turn my lights off. Then, as I went to the front door, it was wide open.

As I walked through the front door into the living room, I was in total shock. Everything was all over the place. My clothes were strewn all over the floor, and my couch was turned upside down on the other side of the room. I looked at the wall: the TV was missing, along with the DVD player.

In a split second, I realized I had just been robbed. I freaked out! My heart started beating out of my chest. This rush of anxiety and uncertainty got the best of me. I'd never been through such a situation. I ran up to my bedroom, and my computer and all my electronics were gone. I continued to go through every single room and found that all my valuables had been taken. Everything was gone. I was devastated.

As I ran back downstairs and into the basement, I saw my back door had been broken into. I didn't know what to do. I thought to myself, what happens if the burglar is still in the house, hiding? I was terrified. I quickly ran out of the house and immediately called 911. The police came shortly after and checked the entire house. Once they said it was safe to go back inside, I filled out a report.

I had lived in this house for over ten years and had always felt safe and secure. Sometimes, I would even leave my door open and had never had an issue. But on this fated day, I was burglarized.

I felt a sense of violation. I'd never had something like that happen to me. I was sad, I was distraught, and I didn't know what to do. At the time, I was having difficulty with my finances, so having my house robbed devastated me.

The next day, I went down to the basement. I had forgotten to check out my safe, which I had hidden in a closet down there. I had some cash and valuables stored in that safe. When I opened the door to the closet, though, the safe was gone, too. I was in total shock! I had about $5,000 in cash inside that safe, and the robbers had taken it *all*. This got me even more down, because I was just starting my online business and money was so tight. Now, all that cash I'd had was gone.

I was in a really rough spot and a very depressed state. As I told my friends and family about what had happened, they consoled me, but there wasn't really much I could do, because I'd been burglarized. In New York, there are a lot of burglaries, so the police really didn't give me any type of solution. They were like, "Oh, we're gonna look into this...," but nothing really happened.

While I was still in shock from this robbery, I called one of my friends with whom I had a business. He didn't pick up the phone, so I left a message. "Hey man, I just got robbed. I wanna talk to you about a lot of stuff."

He didn't get back to me, and I felt something was really off. The next day, I got an email from my friend. He told me that the business we had at the time, which was a personal training business, he'd decided to keep for himself. We had a lot of money tied up in the business, and he just kicked me out of it.

Now I was *severely* screwed, because I did not have a contract. This was a close friend of mine. We had grown this business together from the ground up. We had a verbal agreement, and we were friends. How could he screw me over like that? At this point in time, especially after the robbery, I was even more upset by what he did. How could I have this massive loss and then watch my friend take our business and throw me out, but I couldn't do a thing about it? I was screwed.

So, there I was with this massive violated loss from getting robbed and then my friend robbed me out of our business.

I was so distraught, I felt like I was in a bad nightmare and couldn't get out. I was really sinking low. I said to myself, "What else could happen to me?" I was really upset and felt like there was a string of bad luck or something going on. You know that feeling?

Weeks and weeks passed. I fell into a depression, trying to recover everything. I was trying to figure out how to make some money, plus how to rebuild my life back after being burglarized and having my business taken away from me. I had this fear every single day that something else of mine would be stolen.

I don't know if you've ever been robbed or burglarized, but it's like this violated, unsafe feeling of someone coming up behind you and taking everything you have, while you can't do anything about it. Your home is supposed to be a very sacred place; a safe haven. You know? It is a secure place, and you should feel safe. Now that my home had been burglarized, I had trouble sleeping at night, because I feared they would come back and I would be robbed again or, worse, murdered. I felt my home was not safe any longer.

While I was on the long journey to recuperate and get back to the way life had been, three months after the burglary and loss of my business, on a Friday afternoon, I was at home, working at my computer. It was in the dead of winter and below freezing outside. As I was working, all of a sudden, I smelled smoke. I said to myself, "Okay, this is weird. I'm not cooking anything..."

The smoke odor grew stronger and stronger, and I realized something was burning. I ran upstairs to where my kitchen was and everything seemed fine there.

Then I went upstairs to my bedroom, and all of a sudden, as walked toward that room, I noticed the floors were steaming hot. I knew something was off. Then I looked inside my bedroom and there was smoke coming out of my heater. I realized very quickly there was a fire inside my heating system.

Once again, three months after the burglary, I called 911. "Fire department, there's a fire inside my walls. I need your help!"

I quickly started to panic, because I didn't know what was going to happen: was my house gonna explode? Or would the fire somehow burst through the walls? I remember running outside and looking up. All of a sudden, I could see fire coming out of my bedroom window. Then, my whole house caught on fire.

Luckily, the Fire Department came with axes and hoses, and they knocked down my doors and went inside my house to put out the fire, but by that time it had spread throughout the second floor. There was smoke, water, and damaged debris all over the house. I was devastated.

The fireman on scene said to me, "All right, we got the fire. There was a fire inside the heater, but I'm really, really sorry your house is damaged. You should really stay somewhere else tonight. You can't stay here, because there's a lot of smoke and a lot of debris." There was also no heat.

I remember going inside the house and just staring in disbelief at what had just happened to my comfort place, my home. It had all burned up. Filthy debris and smoke now filled my house. Every room was a mess. Once again, I was beyond devastated. At that moment, in my living room, I literally fell down to my knees and started to cry. I started crying my eyes out because everything I had was gone: from the burglary to the loss of the business to my house burning down. It was the worst moment of my life.

I remember crying and calling my mom. She just said, "Calm down. Everything's gonna be okay. This is all gonna work out."

But all I could think was my life was going to be over. What else was going to happen? Was I going to die? I seemed to be having the very worst luck possible.

After that, I was really sad and distraught, not knowing what else could happen. I went on social media, to Facebook, and I shared everything: the whole story of the burglary, the loss of the business, the house fire. All these wonderful people came out for support. They started checking up on me, texting me, calling me; friends and family from all over. This helped me feel a little bit better. I soon realized that, in hard and devastating times, there are so many people out there to support and encourage me. I felt so blessed.

At the same time as all this was going on, I was in a mastermind group called the 25K Mastermind, run by Joe Polish. They knew what had just happened to me, and they said, "Listen, we have a mastermind meeting next week. I know you're in a really bad place, but I really feel, if you come to this meeting and spend time around your peers, other entrepreneurs, you're gonna be in a much better state. We're gonna come up with a solution for you."

I was going cancel that mastermind meeting because of everything I'd had to do since the fire broke out. There was so much paperwork for the insurance company and the police. But I decided to go—I *needed* to go. So off I went to the mastermind in Phoenix, Arizona in February, one month after the fire.

Joe Polish, the nice gentleman that he is, made me go to the front of the group and share my story: my three months since the burglary and loss of the business, including the house fire, with my house burning down and the devastation that had occurred.

I just stood up and shared my story, becoming really vulnerable. I got very emotional, talking about it, but I had a great sense of relief after I spoke it out loud. Venting was *just* what I needed. I'd never talked about it in a public arena like that.

It was so amazing. Almost every person in that room came up to me after I spoke and congratulated me. They said things like, "You know what? Things are going to get better. This is all happening for a reason." Some recommended books. Some people told me stories of their own losses, including a spouse passing away, a child having cancer, their going bankrupt and losing everything then building it back. And in this mastermind, I was one of the younger guys there. People in their forties, fifties and sixties, shared with me some of the most crazy and devastating things they had ever gone though. I was blown away by that.

After my presentation, they invited me to their masterminds and their events. The fire had happened late January. February was the mastermind, and then, for the next few months, I was invited to all these different events for personal development, marketing, and mindset.

I slowly started to pull myself into that world of rebuilding myself, like a phoenix rising from the ashes. Then I truly realized that all these different entrepreneurs had gone through devastating losses much worse than mine and they had survived. They also said it was the best thing that had ever happened to them. As I was going to these different events, they were sharing stories as well, and I began to feel this crazy, optimistic emotion. I was gonna build my life back. I was gonna make a comeback. And I was gonna change my life.

Over those next few months, I worked really hard, taking lots of action and changing my beliefs. The one thing that kept ringing true to me was, even though my house had been burglarized, I'd lost my business, and my house had burned down, after all these tragedies, I was going to be okay. All these external things were gone, but I was okay. They could take the stuff in my house, but they couldn't take what was inside of me. I could build it all back, as long as I had my health and the right mindset. With those, I am unstoppable.

Being unstoppable became my mantra. I always anchor myself to feeling unstoppable.

Within a few months, I had this newfound confidence. I felt fearless. I believed the worst things that could happen to me had already happened. I realized, whatever else happened, I could handle it. From that moment on, I had this fearless resilience and faith that I could accomplish anything in my path.

I started creating a lot of videos, putting myself out there, doing a lot of fearless actions. And then, all of a sudden, my business started to grow, from $20,000 a month to $40,000 a month, and it kept going up. I felt this amazing confidence, this fearlessness and new energy. This became the most defining moment of my life.

What happened to me was one of the hardest things I have ever had to go through, but it changed my life. What did I learn from that? Essentially, the worst things that happen to you are sometimes the best things that could happen for you. All of the challenges and turmoil were just testing me, making me more resilient, making me more powerful, making me fearless, and then all that.

You have probably gone through something similar, or maybe you're going through something right now. A tragedy, a painful experience, a severe setback. What did you learn from that? Does it make you better or bitter? Right—because we have a choice.

All these things happen externally. Money, material items, a house, shelter. But through it all, my health was okay. I was fine. God forbid, I had a terminal illness. That's a whole other story. The house burned down, yes, but I was okay. I didn't burn. I learned so much from these challenges.

At the end of the day, it's realizing you were put here for a reason. Sometimes, you go through the most challenging, difficult circumstances in order to be taught a life lesson.

Winston Churchill said, "If you're going through hell, keep going." So just keep on persisting. There's sunshine on the other side. That is my advice to you. And that is what really created Online SuperCoach.

A few months after coming out of that negative situation, I created Online SuperCoach as a company to give back: to help people attract their ideal clients, sell their services at the highest level, and serve with their superpowers, because, in that difficult period, I found my superpower and I want to serve you.

So, if you go to my site OnlineSuperCoach.com/start, you can learn more about my program. But I feel so much better sharing this story with you. If you feel you've been inspired by this or know someone who needs to hear this message, please share this with them, because, at the end of the day, the worst thing that could happen to us makes us stronger, makes us wiser, and makes us more resilient.

If you've been inspired by this, I have created a FREE 5-day course on what I have learned, going from rock-bottom to growing a seven-figure online business. You can go here to access it:

https://onlinesupercoach.com/start/

In five days, you will go through the exact framework that has helped me and thousands of my students build their dream online coaching businesses and scale up to six, seven figures and beyond in annual income!

I previously charged $500 for the course, but you can access it for *free,* because you have invested in this book.

Just keep in mind: if you're going through something right now, just keep on going, because something beautiful is on the other side.

###

ABOUT AJ MIHRZAD: *AJ is the author of the best-selling book,* The Mind Body Solution: Train your Brain for Permanent Weight Loss. *He studied Exercise Science and Nutrition because of his passion for health, and earned a master's degree in psychology, which developed his fascination with the mindset of weight loss. His cutting-edge approach to permanent weight loss insists that the key to a healthy body is a healthy brain. His clients are walking proof this is true: there are hundreds of them!*

AJ was recently inducted into the Personal Trainer Hall of Fame. His writing has also been featured in Entrepreneur Magazine, The Huffington Post, Men's Fitness, *and* Bodybuilding.com. *AJ is a keynote speaker at high-end entrepreneurial and personal development events. He is also the host of the popular podcast, the* Online SuperCoach Podcast, *available on iTunes. Along with inspiring the lives of the general public, he is dedicated to helping coaches create an ethical and profitable online income through his business mentorship program, available at OnlineSuperCoach.com.*

From Corporate Captive to Motivated Maven

JENN SCALIA

THE NEW YEAR is a time for celebration and reinvention. Most people make resolutions and promises to themselves. I was no different. I was elated and had a feeling of joy, thinking of all the things I was going to do this upcoming year. I was especially ecstatic about my new career. I had just taken a job at a high-profile casino and resort in Atlantic City, in a new position within the marketing department.

I went into work the day after New Year's and was totally motivated. I got in early, started my work, and had made serious headway in my first two hours. Then I was asked to come into my boss's office, which was usually no big deal. We had a great relationship, and I was hoping for some good news.

But when the door shut, I knew something wasn't right. I was asked to take a seat. And, being the rebel I was, of course I didn't. I knew what was going on and felt instantly devastated. My family was just getting back on their feet financially, after I had taken off two years for maternity leave and stayed home with my son. Now, my household income was being viciously slashed in half.

I was completely discouraged and destroyed. At thirty-two years old, I was still trying to figure out what I wanted to do with my life. I spent almost two full months in my sweatpants, feeling sorry for myself. Every day, I was told by my parents, my husband, and everyone around me that I needed to get out there and look for a "job." But I knew in my heart there was no way I was ever going back to a *JOB*. I made a conscious decision to never be a slave to the nine-to-five again.

For me, life was too short to continue living someone else's dream. I knew I needed to do something drastic in order to live the life I'd always wanted and to have complete freedom over my life and finances. With zero income, $50,000 of debt, and plain old fear and doubt weighing me down, I made a decision to invest in myself. Within a few short months, I became focused and clear. I found my calling in life and was able to create a profitable business encompassing my passion. I'm telling you this because I want you to know, no matter where you are in your life, you can always move past it and live your dreams. It all starts with *YOU*.

Whether you are unemployed, in a job you don't necessarily love, or thinking about starting your own business, it's time to focus on your goals and dreams and stop being a slave to Mr. Paycheck. All too often, work and what we really love doing are two very different things. In fact, the vast majority of the world does not enjoy their work. If you find yourself out of a job as a result of a layoff, maternity leave, or some other unexpected circumstance, this becomes an opportunity for reinvention toward a more fulfilling career path. It may seem like a huge shock at first and will take some getting used to, but it will eventually bring you closer to your true destiny, if that's what you so desire.

Most people have to wait to acquire vacation time or PTO in order to be able to go out there and do what they truly love. We often dream up ideas that get us excited and motivated, but, the majority of the time, we fail to act upon them. Fear and/or doubt hold us back. We emphasize practicality over passion, and we concentrate on being responsible, paying bills, and doing what we are *supposed* to do. Routines are an easy trap to fall into and can rob years off our lives.

If you are truly ready to get unstuck, you must become really introspective and honest with yourself. Your change in direction will be guided largely by your attitude and determination to succeed, despite the doom and gloom on the headline news. Each and every one of us has the skills needed to succeed. It's just a matter of how you utilize them. Having someone there to guide you and hold you accountable can help you get you off on the right foot the first time. Remember: you only get one chance to make a first impression. A coach or mentor can help guide you on the right path.

Sure, you can read tons of career books, watch webinars, and take online courses, but if you don't have anyone holding you accountable, you may be hard-pressed to actually apply it all to your situation. Creating a new life requires clear direction and is not easy by any stretch of the imagination. But if you want something—really want it—you can make it happen.

Being stuck and confused are costlier now than any other time in history. You must think creatively. You must work smarter (not harder). And you must admit there are some things you just can't do all by yourself. Keep in mind that using a coach or enrolling in courses will cost money, so you must be willing to invest in yourself. I mean really, wholeheartedly invest in yourself. Not your body or your image, but your mind, your brand, and your business. Educate yourself and smother yourself in knowledge about your chosen field. Having an abundance of knowledge gives you the confidence and edge to go after what you really want. It gives you leverage in your field and, ultimately, in your business or career.

This could be one of the most important steps you take in your life or business. You absolutely must invest in yourself. I know what you're thinking: "I don't have the money" or "I don't have the time," but if you really want it, you will find a way. Start looking at it as capital investment, not debt. Bottom line is, whatever you decide to do, you can't half-ass it. You're going to have to invest in your own education and professional endeavors.

Promise yourself to only work with the best and expect only the best. Don't ever compromise quality. If you want to really rock it as an aspiring entrepreneur, you're going to have to shell out some *dinero*—whether it's on certifications, marketing, hiring employees, or just keeping things running. And please, please, please: Do your research! The Internet will put you on information overdrive. You have to be smart about your decisions. Make sure you are investing in products and services that are accredited and in line with your personal values. The most successful people say "no" to the good things so they can say "yes" to the best things.

I coach people every day to become self-motivators. I've seen how paralyzing it is not to do what you love in business and in life. And as you know from my story, *I'VE BEEN THERE*. I believe everyone is powerful—some of us are just too fearful to go out and get it. It's my job to show you how to become the superstar you were born to be, grow your business, and design the life of your dreams.

The goal is to help you identify the good habits that will move your life forward and the bad habits that are holding you back. Moreover, you need an accountability partner to provide the necessary guidance and support your need to facilitate your goals. You're not stuck where you are, unless you want to be. Just know the right choices can bring you abundant wealth and happiness.

Nine times out of ten, the solution is right at your fingertips, but fear could be blinding you from seeing it. I want you get really clear on what you most need to do right now, to move to the next level in your life and business quickly and easily. If you are an entrepreneur in particular, you will need to devote time to bettering yourself, if you want to be successful in your endeavor.

If you feel like you have a burning desire or untapped potential that you've been unable to grasp or develop, a career coach can help you discover aspects of personal development, including setting realistic and tangible goals, self-motivation, changing habits, improving self-awareness, and identifying your values and beliefs.

Successful people don't make decisions based on money; they make decisions based on their goals. And wouldn't you be happier, living the life you truly want, instead of the one you are *supposed* to live?

I've put together a series of questions and action steps to get you started on your journey from corporate captive to motivated maven. Head over to: jennscalia.com/innergame. Take a look at the action steps. *Oh!* And actually *DO* them. Grab a pen and paper, and let's discover where your passion lies *NOW*... Answer the questions honestly, and really dig deep. You will find the right answers.

I strongly encourage you to take action quickly, while you're excited and motivated. What steps will you commit to taking within one week, to move you toward your dream? I'd love to hear from you. And if you need someone to hold you accountable, I'd be more than happy to do it. Just shoot me an email at: inspire@jennscalia.com and tell me your story.

And finally, check out my best-selling book on how to make six figures doing what you love:

www.yourfirstsixfigures.com.

###

ABOUT JENN SCALIA: *Jenn is a visibility strategist and mindset mentor for entrepreneurs who want to make an impact. She is THE go-to expert for entrepreneurs who want the world to know their name. This self-professed introvert and single mom went from rock-bottom to creating a seven-figure business within three years. Known for her tough-love, no-B.S. style, Jenn helps entrepreneurs overhaul their biggest fears and empowers them to share their message with the world. She is the CEO and Mastermind of Million Dollar Mommy, a company founded to help women across the world reach their dreams and financial goals. Jenn has been featured in* Business Insider, Inc. *and* Forbes.com. *She is also the best-selling author of* Your First Six Figures: 8 Keys to Unlock Freedom, Flow and Financial Success with Your Online Business.

Failure is Not the Opposite of Success... It's Part of the Process Untitled

JONO PETROHILOS

I WAS TWENTY-SEVEN years old. I'd had a good childhood and grew up in a high-socioeconomic area. My parents were successful. My mum was a psychologist; my dad was high up in the education system. They were still together. I went to a private school, was well educated, and went to university.

But at twenty-seven years old, I felt like an absolute loser. All my friends were getting married, having kids, starting successful careers, moving into their own places, and buying houses. I was living with my parents. I was single, had no kids, and had a low-paying job. I was a university-educated exercise physiologist, but I was working full-time on a gym floor.

You might be reading this and thinking, "He's got full-time work. That's okay."

Look, it *was* okay, but it wasn't what I'd gotten into the health and fitness industry to do. I had thought I was going to be helping people: doing studies, rehab, cardiac rehab, weight loss, and strength training. But no. I was spending most of my day cleaning treadmills, re-racking the dumbbells or the soda machine, and doing the bathroom checks.

I even had to do *this* one job: trim the carpet hairs... I kid you not. When the carpet hairs on the floor got too long, it was apparently a safety hazard, so I had to get down on my hands and knees with the scissors and cut those carpet hairs. That was one of the most demeaning things I've ever done in my life.

The one good part about the job was I did get to meet a lot of people, but some of the conversations just went the wrong way. People would say, "Hey, what do you do, apart from this?"

I was, like, "Oh, well, this is actually my full-time job."

They'd say, "Okay, but isn't the money's crap?" Or, "Oh, okay, so are you working here full-time and then studying something else on the side?"

I had to reply, "No, I've actually already studied. I'm a qualified exercise physiologist."

They'd be, like, "Wow, you're a qualified exercise physiologist... What are you doing here...?"

That stuff really affected me.

I had to lie to my friends, too... They'd ask, "How's work?"

And I'd have to basically lie to their face and say, "Yeah, it's good. I'm just plugging away," because anything that came out of my mouth that wasn't, "My job sucks! I'm a university-educated exercise physiologist, and I'm cleaning treadmills for a full-time job," was a lie...

I knew, on this salary, I was not going to be able to get married and raise a family; I couldn't afford to pay for a wedding and buy a place. So, I knew this wasn't for me, but I didn't know the answer. Honestly, what I thought at that stage was, "Hey, I've just got to keep doing what I'm doing, and, sooner or later, somebody's going to come along and offer me a cushy job where I don't have to do much but I'll make a lot of money." That's how I thought the world worked.

I found out pretty quickly it wasn't, but it's an interesting story about how I did find that out...

One day, I saw an ad on the Internet that read, "Hey, you're a qualified personal trainer? Well, hey, come and work with our franchise. Most of our trainers make over $75,000 a year working 60 minutes a day."

I was, like, "Hold on. I'm not even making half that much mone,y and I'm working eight, nine hours a day. I don't even like my job. I'm going all-out on this."

I applied for the job. I bumbled my way through it and did the usual, exaggerated on my résumé, but I actually got a "trial." The head of the franchise said they were going to come to Sydney and watch one of my bootcamp sessions. But there was a little issue. I actually wasn't running any bootcamp sessions at the time (although I mentioned I was, in my résumé...).

Lucky for me, I was covering someone's boxing class for three weeks. I thought that was perfect. They could come down and watch me on my third boxing class.

Luckily it was the third, because my first two classes were absolute rubbish. They were so bad, I got complaints. I was considering even just pulling out of this interview, because I figured the third one could be an embarrassment" But I thought, "No, no, no. This is the dream job. This is what I've been looking for. I'm going to put the effort in and I'm going to do it."

So I ran the session and it was actually pretty good, right? It was definitely the best session I'd ever run, and I got the job. I said to myself, "Hey, dream come true."

But there was one issue. I sucked at this job. I got the job, but I sucked at it. Surprise, surprise, right? I sucked at the job I'd lied to get... And man was I bad. Basically, you were ranked on your retention. Let's say the franchise gave you twenty clients. Your job was to get those clients to come back, and then they'd give you another few clients, so you could build from there. That's how you would grow your income.

Unfortunately, I wasn't able to do that, because I sucked. This is how bad I was. There were seventy-five different locations across Australia, New Zealand, and the USA. Take a guess at what I was ranked? If you guessed seventy-five, you were right. And I'm competitive. If I come in second at something, I'm upset. If I come in third at something, I'm very, very upset. If I come fourth at something, it's borderline depression. I came in seventy-fifth, all right?

What's worse was I knew the trainer who came in seventy-fourth, and I thought they were the worst trainer I'd ever seen. But they smoked me. That's the level I was at. I was better at keeping the stats at how bad I was than actually running the bootcamp, and that says something. Anyway, there was an end-of-year convention for this company, and all the trainers had to attend.

I didn't want to go, because I was a self-conscious as it was. As a personal trainer, I wasn't the biggest, I wasn't the strongest, I wasn't the smartest, I wasn't the sexiest. On top of that, I was already a bit self-conscious. But on top of *that*, I was the worst trainer there. It's not that I thought I was the worst trainer there. It was that I'd been statistically proven the worst trainer there.

I knew, if I went up there, it would prove that. It would prove, "Hey, you're the worst trainer here." So, I really didn't want to go, but I thought, "Hey, if I don't go, I'm going to get fired. If I go, maybe I'll get fired, but maybe I won't, so I better go."

Well, I went. And it was actually the best thing I've ever done. This particular conference was half about how to be a better trainer, but half of it was just personal development.

The "how to be a better trainer "part, yes, I got a lot out of it. But I was already doing a little bit of that, anyway. The personal development side of things, though, I'd never even heard of that material.

I still remember this clearly, because the head of the franchise was going to come down to Sydney and attend Tony Robbins's convention. He said, "Hey, is anyone down to go to this Tony Robbins convention?"

I think tickets were... oh, it was at least $1,000. I looked at that and said, "What the hell? $1000 for a two-day convention, and it's not even fitness-based. This person's going to tell me how to reach my goals and get motivated? No way am I going to that." But at the end of this conference, I was just fascinated.

I spoke to the head of the franchise and asked, "Hey, how do you know all this stuff? All this personal development stuff?"

He told me, "Well, look, I study a lot into personal development. I do all the Tony Robbins stuff. I've read all the books. I really believe that's why I'm in the position I'm in."

I also spent a lot of time at the convention speaking to the more successful trainers there. The amount of education these trainers did was ridiculous. I did the bare minimum to stay in the industry. Basically, to stay in the industry, you need to do a continuing education course on fitness every year, to keep your accreditation.

I did that. But these successful trainers, they were doing four or five different courses a year. It just flipped my mind! I asked, "Why are you doing that much? You only need to do one."

They said, "Yeah, but I want to be the best at what I do. I want to get ahead. One's just not enough."

I thought, "All right, cool. Instead of me doing one a year, I'm going to do one a quarter."

I decided I was going to open my mind to this personal development stuff. I got some recommendations and read all of *Rich Dad Poor Dad* the *How to Win Friends and Influence People*, and Napoleon Hill's *Think and Grow Rich*. All of those sorts of books there.

I saw my bootcamp just grow and grow and grow. Not so much from the actual exercise side of things; more from the personal development side of things. Yeah, my training got a little bit better, but it was my personal development that really helped take me to that next level.

To cut a long story short, after investing in myself more and doing all the personal development, like going to the seminars, reading the books, and also implementing the action, one year after that first convention, I went back.

I wasn't ranked seventy-fifth. I was actually ranked number one! So, 75 to 1 in one year. That wasn't it for me, though. That was good in its own, but I thought, "Hey, I don't just want to be the best instructor in this franchise. I want to be the best bootcamp instructor in the world."

I went out there and just kept doing what I'm doing. Now, if we fast forward a few years, I've put together an online course for other personal trainers who want to grow their bootcamp, laying out here's the things you do. That's now my full-time job and it's making me multiple six figures a year. I do that online, working from home.

I put this all down to personal development. My suggestion to you reading this is to invest in yourself. You don't spend money on personal development. You invest money.

Let's say I do a twelve-week business coaching or a twelve-week personal development course that costs me $500. Beautiful. I make my $500 back within that twelve weeks, but, ideally, I've got the knowledge to make at least an extra $500 every quarter for the rest of my life

So now, instead of getting fifty leads, you're getting two hundred leads. Instead of getting four or five sales, you're getting fifteen, twenty 20 sales, or whatever it may be, okay? And that's how you grow your business. It's the same with your personal development. If you do that $500 personal-development course and by the end of the year you've got an extra $1,500 because of it, don't just blow that money, next time instead of doing the $500 course, you do the $1,500 course and you'll grow from there.

The more you invest in yourself, the more successful you're going to be. That's my takeaway there.

Get in touch with Jono:

Facebook: www.facebook.com/jono.petrohilos

Instagram: @jono_petrohilos

ABOUT JONO PETROHILOS: *A qualified exercise physiologist and personal trainer, Jono is currently the director at Fitness Education Online, one of the largest online providers of continuing education courses for personal trainers in the world, and the host of the podcast "The Bootcamp Blueprint: The Place Where Personal Trainers Go to Grow their Bootcamp and Social Media."*

Fearless Faith:
Transforming Pain into Power

CAT ALMANZOR

IT WAS TWO YEARS of the highest highs and lowest lows. I wanted to give up at times, but I didn't have a choice. I had two little ones who were watching me. I had to be strong and show them that it would be okay.

I didn't have a choice....

Spring had finally arrived. The pastel-colored flowers were blooming, and the air was fresh and crisp. It's my favorite season. As I sat at my cubicle at work, my phone started ringing. I had an unusual urge to answer it. When I said, "Hello," the police department on the other end.

The policeman asked, "Are you aware that your daughter has been harmed?"

I almost fell out my chair. From that moment, I had no idea my life would completely change forever. That summer was filled with pain and sadness. My marriage of twelve years, to a man I'd been with since I was a teenager, crumbled by end of the year. But, together, we fought for justice for my daughter, and by the next spring, we had victory.

But it was still rough, the divorce process was ugly and went sour. I was in pain from his infidelity and cried myself to sleep, asking myself if I could've done something different. I was scared, as well. I had not ever been on my own financially and was also taking care of my parents. I wondered how I would move on with my life.

Somehow, something inside of me just clicked. I told myself, I can do this. I had to pull through. I was more than enough.

I focused on bettering and loving myself first. I felt for a little bit, but then, by summer time, my grandma, who'd raised me in the Philippines, fell ill. I had planned to visit her every year but kept putting it off. I knew I would regret it, if I didn't go. So, I went. When I arrived in the Philippines, she passed away the very next day, as if she'd been waiting for me.

I was heartbroken. This person had molded me into who I am today. I didn't have time to process everything that was happening. It was one thing after another, and I started just going through the motions.

I arrived back at the States with mixed emotions, feeling as if I was getting ready for something else traumatic to happen. A I went back to work a couple days of later, but I felt uneasy and couldn't quite figure out what was happening to me.

One of my co-workers told me it was stress, and I agreed with her. But later that day, I couldn't find where I'd parked. Then I had headache. By that weekend, I also had a migraine, but I thought it was all due to jet lag after traveling time different zones and my lack of sleep. Boy, I was so wrong!

That night, I had insomnia. I was up at 3 a.m., sobbing, and I couldn't control my sadness. I had repetitive music running through my head and thoughts I couldn't control. I was scared as hell, aware that something was wrong with me.

The next day, as I went for coffee with my co-worker, I started hallucinating. I saw Superman walking toward me. I wanted to tell my co-worker, but I was afraid she was going think I was crazy. I went on with my day, but then had a breakdown in the woman's bathroom by noon.

I was sitting in the toilet as tears flowed down my face, asking myself, "Am I too young for a midlife crisis?" I couldn't control my emotions. I sat in the stall until my friend came in to rescue me. A couple of hours later, I was sent home in a taxi, as it was obvious I was not making any sense and needed to get help.

Everything went downhill when I arrived at the emergency room. I sat at the lobby, waiting to be called, and looked at the television. I became afraid: it was speaking to me directly! What did I do? Did I do something wrong? I looked at everyone in the room and felt as they were all staring at me. Then I got up to go to the bathroom, for some relief, but I could hear the hospital communication system stating they were looking for me, as if I had escaped. I stood there, waiting for someone to get me, but no one came.

The next thing I remember, I was waiting in a hospital room. The nurse asked me a few questions, and I was mad at myself for not knowing the answers. I was aware I'd given her the wrong answers, but I couldn't remember when she asked me where I worked, what I did, and when was my birthday. I thought, *How do I not know these basic things?* I laid on the sterile bed in a fetal position, thinking I was going to die. This is the end, I told myself.

Then the nurse came back with a couple of medics. They strapped me on a stretcher and wheeled me away to an ambulance. I could see the red lights flashing and, suddenly, I closed my eyes.

I "woke" up three months later. I had no recollection of anything that had transpired. I thought I was dreaming the whole time. It took intense physical, occupational, and speech therapy to get me back to whatever my normal meant.

I will never forget the day when one the doctors showed me an image and asked me what it was. It was picture of a hammer. I knew what it was. But the word wouldn't come out of my mouth. It was not translating to my brain. I was so frustrated with myself, and I was scared I would not be able speak correctly ever again.

On the very first day I was wheeled out in a wheelchair, to practice walking outside the hospital, the sun was shining so bright. The sound of the cars driving by affected me, too. I stood up on the wheelchair and took my first steps. I was embarrassed: everyone was looking at me. Taking a shower was an ordeal, too. I fell in the tub several times, but then I forced myself to get back up on my own every single time. I refused to give up.

To this day, I still don't have a definite diagnosis, because I opened my eyes while doctors were trying variations of treatments. The closest diagnosis is anti-NMDA receptor encephalitis, which is a type of brain inflammation due to antibodies.

Over the next few months, I devoted myself every single day to learning how to walk again. My dad walked with me at the mall every single morning, alongside the elderly. My left leg was still slightly bent and I couldn't straighten it. I had to exercise my brain, as well, so I purchased elementary-level workbooks so I could relearn basic math and writing. I also had to pass a driving test again. I cried when I drove on the highway for the very first time. I had to relearn every single thing all over again, but it was worth it. I wouldn't change a thing. Everything that happened to me gave a different meaning to my life.

My kids were affected the most. They thought they had lost me. I couldn't have pulled through without the help of my family and friends. I'm so lucky to have an amazing support system. I was given another chance at life and vowed not to take it lightly. Within my first year of returning back to the real world, I've done more with my life than I did in my entire life before the hospitalization and traumatic recovery process. Something changed in me, and I came back stronger than ever.

I've had to rebuild my life and pick up the pieces as a single mom, in order to raise my two kids. The back-to-back tragedies served as a catalyst for me to create a life of purpose and joy. Loving myself was the first step. Fully knowing who I am as person and what I'm capable of gave me confidence in how I live my life.

I'm now an active kickboxer, half-marathon runner, and in the best shape of my life, after losing almost forty pounds. I'm in control of my finances and my future, and I even found my soul mate. I became more confident after revealing my authentic self with no fear, and I've excelled in my career.

I've learned you heal when you share your story. The more you reveal, the better you heal. You don't need to have it all figured out to move forward. Take it one step at time, but don't be afraid to lean in on others. As human beings, we have the innate power to build each other up. I'm building a community of warriors who refuse to give up. I'm now pursuing my calling to empower other women to walk with purpose and transform their pain into power.

As a way to say thank you for purchasing this book, I'm offering a free *gift: 8 Steps Guide to Reveal, Heal and Transform Your Pain into Power.*

Send an email to catalmanzorSheHeals@gmail.com.

ABOUT CAT ALMANZOR: *Cat is a transformational life coach for the mind, body, and spirit. Her mission in life is to equip women to transform pain into power. She partners with women after experiencing toxic relationships, traumatic experiences, or severe life stressors.*

Cat has known defeat, suffering, struggle, and loss, and she has found her way out of those depths. It was a back-to-back life tragedy that served as a painful catalyst for Cat to create a life of pure purpose and joy. After a divorce, fighting for justice for her daughter, being hospitalized for three months, after which she had to re-learn everything, and the death of her grandma, who raised her, she was pushed to take control of her life.

She is passionate about empowering women to walk with purpose and stand in their authentic unique identity.

Cat is a single mom to two teenagers, a brain injury survivor and warrior, a social-media guru, investor, and kickboxer. She grew up in a small province in the Philippines and currently resides in Seattle, Washington.

Instagram: https://www.instagram.com/shehealswithpurpose/

Facebook: https://www.facebook.com/shehealswithpurpose/

From Unsustainable to Unboxed:
Releasing the Weight of Limiting Beliefs to Thrive

MARY ALLISON BROWN

A LITTLE VOICE deep inside of me kept whispering, "This is unsustainable."

I tried to ignore it, but it just grew louder. No matter what I did, happiness, joy, and fulfillment remained elusive—always just out of my reach. Meanwhile, the voice kept getting louder and more persistent, while I did my best not to listen.

Until I got a text message that forced me to pay attention.

> *He has dulled your sparkle, and you're finally starting to get it back now. You have to decide if he fits into a world in which you are exactly* **you**, *every single day.*

When I read that message, it felt like being punched in the gut. I couldn't breathe.

I knew I couldn't avoid it any longer. I was at a crossroads and had to make a choice.

I wanted desperately *not* to have to make a choice. I wished, in vain, everything could just somehow be okay again. Except, even as I had the thought, I knew I was lying to myself. Had things really *ever* been okay?

The truth is the life I had built for myself was never really right for me from the beginning. It was like a house of cards: built on a foundation that was becoming more unstable by the minute and all threatening to come tumbling down.

How had I allowed myself to get so far off course?

As a child, I felt unloved and unlovable. My earliest journals are filled with themes of feeling alone, misunderstood, angry, and disconnected. As a teenager, I sought validation and connection wherever I could. My first relationship quickly turned abusive.

I remember one incident when my high-school boyfriend screamed at me to "Shut the fuck up!" and shoved me backwards into a door, right in front of my father. My father, the person whom I most expected to unconditionally love and protect me, did not. He looked directly at me, eyes wide, and said, "Be careful, Mary Allison." Then he watched me walk out of the house and get into a car with an angry, aggressive teenage boy.

In that moment, I learned I wasn't worthy of love and protection. Over time, that belief became so strong, it shaped all of my decisions and behaviors.

And then, at seventeen, I was raped. I was so angry at myself and ashamed of my inability to keep myself safe. Even when rumors began and I was bullied at school, I never told anyone what had really happened. Instead, I buried all of the pain and fear deep within my soul. For nearly twenty years, I believed the rape was my own fault, and I carried the crushing burdens of shame and guilt. When any uncomfortable emotions threatened to approach the surface, I did whatever I had to do to push them back down as quickly as possible.

I eventually lost track of who I was altogether, so I tried desperately to be whomever it was I thought other people wanted me to be. I started drinking as much as possible, to numb my uncomfortable emotions and to mask my insecurities. Drinking and drugs quickly became social crutches. When I was drunk or high, nothing else mattered and I could just forget about all the ways my soul was hurting.

A few years later, I experienced a particularly challenging stretch of time. I found myself withdrawing from friends, neglecting my schooling, and just going through the motions at work. It got serious enough that, one day, a co-worker offered to drive me home. On the drive, she expressed her concern and offered her help. She had been depressed, too, she told me.

I remember feeling both completely surprised and in denial (I wasn't depressed!), but also an overwhelming sense of relief that someone had noticed. I was drowning inside, but, in that conversation, it was like someone had thrown me a life raft. I grasped onto it with everything I had and, very slowly, began to pull myself out of the water.

Shortly after that conversation, just as the fog was beginning to lift from my life, my parents came to visit me. After several glasses of wine, my mother accused me of being on drugs. While I had certainly done my fair share of partying and experimenting, during that particular time it wasn't really a part of my life. I was depressed.

The irony of her slurred words as she accused me across the table was not lost on me. I got so fucking angry. How dare she get wasted and then accuse *me* of being on drugs? How dare she not notice that something was actually really, truly wrong?! I stormed out.

My dad followed me and confronted me on the street. True to our dysfunctional but highly consistent family patterns, I cried and directed all of my anger for my mother at him. Also true to our family patterns, he defended her relentlessly and made excuses for her behavior. Once again, I felt completely unworthy of protection, unloved, and unlovable.

In what I now recognize as an act of self-preservation, I bought a one-way ticket from Boston to San Diego. I think I believed San Diego would be an opportunity to break away from my past, so I could finally become the person I was meant to be.

Instead, San Diego just gave me more people to try to impress. By the time I was twenty-three, I had become a shell of a person, with nothing to hold onto. I had unceremoniously lost every last bit of my authentic identity. I had become all façade, no substance. I'd buried the wisdom of my own inner guidance so far underneath all the things I'd picked up, in an attempt to make sense of who I was, that I couldn't hear anything it was trying to tell me.

When I met my husband, I ignored the warning signs that we weren't right for each other and stubbornly forced our relationship to work as best I could. I was so desperate to prove I was worthy of love, I settled for something that looked close enough, from the outside.

I replaced the drugs and alcohol with other unhealthy coping mechanisms. I found myself relentlessly hustling for my worthiness and seeking external validation. I was constantly running toward an invisible finish line to somehow prove to the world—and myself—once and for all that I was worthy of love and protection.

For twenty years, I built my life on a foundation of beliefs that I wasn't worthy of love and protection, that I was unloved and unlovable. I missed out on so many things because I was paralyzed by self-doubt and desperately avoided any genuine emotions.

And then, I received the text message that turned my world upside down.

When I read that text, I knew I had to make a choice, no matter how much I didn't want to. It felt like a choice between willingly plunging my life and the lives of my children into complete chaos or letting my soul die.

By then, I was much stronger than I had been in the past. I knew I could face this challenge and come out on the other side. I decided I could no longer live in a world in which I had to be anything other than exactly who I was, every single day. I chose me and my soul over everything else.

I was exhausted from a lifetime of trying to cram myself into boxes I didn't really fit into in the first place. I was being crushed by the weight of guilt and shame that was never mine to carry. For the first time, I allowed myself to see my past trauma and adversity for what it really was.

Since the day I received that text message, my life has changed dramatically. There have been tears and grief, but also more joy than I could have imagined. There has been massive growth and transformation.

I have learned the only way to move past deep emotional pain is to dig deep and allow ourselves to feel it. I have learned how to listen to my own inner guidance, to set strong boundaries to protect my heart and energy, and to stand strong in who I am. In doing so, I have set myself free. I have finally released the anchors that had been holding me back, so I can now lean into the wind and see how high I can truly soar.

If you know that fear, limiting beliefs, or past traumas have been holding you back from stepping fully into the life you're meant to lead, I'd love to chat. Come visit me at www.maryallisonbrown.com. You'll find a free offer designed to help you recognize and release the things that hold you back, so you, too, can accomplish all of your big, bold goals.

###

ABOUT MARY ALLISON BROWN: *Mary Allison is an author, speaker, mental health therapist, and mindset and empowerment coach. Mary Allison has always been a helper at heart, which led her to earn her master's degree in social work. She believes each of us is here on purpose and, in order to step fully into that purpose, we must shift our relationship with fear, stop self-sabotaging, and own our worthiness. Mary Allison used to live a life ruled by limiting beliefs and fear, but she's since learned how to believe fully in her worth, instead.*

Her favorite part of coaching is combining her background in neuroscience and mental health therapy with spiritual practice and principles to create life-changing magic. *Mary Allison believes our thoughts shape our lives and intentionally focusing on joy and gratitude is a game-changer. She is the author of* Align With Joy: A 30-Day Guided Joy Journal Designed to Help You Cultivate a Life Filled With Joy and Gratitude. *Mary Allison enjoys learning as much as possible, spending time with her two daughters, running, yoga, and mastering new tricks on the flying trapeze.*

Let Fear Be Your Compass

VITALE BUFORD

I WALK INTO THE DOORWAY of my boss's office. He's on the phone, his phone pinched between his right ear and his shoulder, and he's staring at his computer.

He senses someone at his door, looks up at me with a smile, and, with a nod of his head, signals for me to come in and sit down. His office is decorated like any lawyer's office: diplomas and awards and law books perfectly in place. As I sit down in one of his office chairs, I can tell his mind is occupied with ten different projects. He's the Managing Partner of the law firm, so, of course, he's busy.

As I'm sitting in the chair, I feel my body tighten and my chest clench. I cross my arms, because I'm nervous and scared and, honestly, don't know what to do with them. I have no idea what words I'm going to use to tell him my news. I have no clue how he will react.

I play the conversation over and over in my head—maybe a million times. In one scene, he fires me after I break the news to him. In another scenario, he is overly understanding, and we hug. I don't know which one it will be: the first, second, or somewhere in between. Part of me wants him to stay on the phone forever, and part of me wants to get this conversation over immediately, just rip the Band-Aid off.

I close my eyes and ask God for the strength to make it through the next few minutes. I hope I don't pass out. I hope I don't have a heart attack in his perfectly upholstered office chair. The outcome of this conversation will determine the course of my life.

He hangs up his phone, and, suddenly, I feel my throat tighten. My hands are sweating and I am shaking. My hands tremble so terribly, I put my blue pen down on my pad of paper, so he can't tell how bad it is.

This is it. This is the scariest moment of my life. I have no idea how the next few minutes will play out. I feel like I'm going to throw up.

My mind is all over the place, racing from one thought to the next. What will he say? What will he think? Can he tell I'm nervous? Does he know what I'm about to tell him? How will he react?

All these questions play over and over in my mind as he looks up from his computer, greets me by name, and asks me how I'm doing and how he can help me. Which I find amusing—because he has no idea what I'm about to tell him.

All I can think is I'm about to lose my job, which will be the end of the world. I want to curl up in a ball and not exist. I want to disappear.

I respond to his questions, and then say, "Sir, I need to tell you something."

He responds with a joyful, "Okay," but, honestly, he has no idea what's about to hit him. His entire opinion of me is going to change in the next few minutes. I'm about go from the Super Amazing Marketing & Business Development Director of a high-powered law firm to a lowly prescription drug addict who needs to go to rehab.

"Sir, I have something I need to tell you, and this is probably the most difficult conversation I've ever had." He looks at me confused but gestures for me to continue. "I have an addiction to Adderall, and I need to go to rehab." I say it quickly, so I can't take it back. I have admitted out loud to the managing partner that I'm addicted to prescription drugs. There's no going back now. My life flashes before my eyes. I have a sinking feeling in my stomach and my chest is tight.

He pauses for what feels like an eternity. I am anxious for his response. To my surprise, he reacts to my news warmly. He asks me several questions about my addiction, and I answer all of them. I explain how long I've been addicted to the drug and that I want to change my life. He happily gives me the two weeks off I request for rehab.

I think to myself, *That was it? All of that freaking out for nothing?* I walk out of his office and feel lighter. The truth is out there, and I can't take it back. Thank God. I can't take back my public admission of the truth. My shoulders feel lighter. I've been addicted to Adderall for ten years, and I'm finally doing something about it. This is a defining moment in my life. I've done something scary and lived to tell about it.

I walk out of the office that day and drive myself to in-patient rehab. I have no idea what to expect, but since I just survived the scariest conversation of my life, I trust I can make it through fourteen days of rehab.

The next two weeks of sobriety turn into thirty days, then six months, then four years.

Getting sober was my rebirth and my awakening. For these purposes, we will call my sobriety my "new life," because it marks the start of a new way of living. I am where I am today because I let fear be my guide. All of my growth is measured by the number of scary things I've been willing to do. Here are some of the scary things I've walked through in my new life:

Six months into my new life, I developed an eating disorder. I was afraid of gaining weight, losing control, and not being enough. All I thought about was when I could work out and what I was going to eat. It consumed my life, just like Adderall had. After a year of disordered eating, I woke up one day and decided enough is enough. I had allowed Adderall to control my life, and I was now allowing food and body image to control my life.

I stepped into my fear and out of my comfort zone and stopped restricting my foods. I started using affirmations to help me make a mental shift with my body image. I let fear guide me out of disordered eating into a healthier relationship with food. Food and exercise no longer run my life—they are just now parts of my life.

Two years into my new life, I became the guardian of my seven-year-old nephew, Ben. I was a single, independent woman living my life for myself who looked beyond myself for the first time and realized I could give Ben a sober, healthy home to grow up in. A home I'd never had.

Going from being a single, self-focused woman to a single mom was a scary change. But I allowed fear to guide me toward it instead of run from it. And I'm so grateful, because he changed me and my life in ways I could never have imagined. We are healing together.

Three-and-a-half years into my new life, I decided to leave the comfort of my full-time corporate job to become a full-time entrepreneur. I had no money in savings or on credit cards. All I had was faith in myself. I'd built my courage muscle up during my new life, so I was willing and ready to take the daunting leap set in front of me.

I was called to step into my purpose and teach women to transform their lives. I let fear guide me out of the comfort of a full-time salary into the unknown of entrepreneurship. Owning a business takes courage every single day, and I'm so grateful to do it, because now I get to help women change their lives every single day. When you find your purpose, it's worth taking the leap.

These are just a few examples of how I've followed my fear and allowed it to change me. You can do big scary things and you can do small scary things. They all require the same amount of courage and belief in yourself.

If you have an unhealthy relationship, you can follow your fear by having that difficult conversation you've been avoiding or even by ending the relationship.

If you have a career that makes you unhappy, you can follow your fear by applying for other jobs.

If you have a lack of work/life balance, you can follow your fear by saying no to certain things or setting aside time just for yourself.

You must have faith you can do scary things. And even though you may experience growing pains—it's worth it. You must believe in yourself and believe that facing your fears will change you.

When you get a hint of fear creeping in, get curious. Let it guide you. Be willing to walk through the discomfort and the pain and the fear to get to the other side. Because the other side is way better than you could have ever imagined. Walking through my fear led me to my purpose.

So, the next time you are faced with something scary, trust that it is the path to bigger and better things. Let fear be your compass. It has changed the course of my life, and it can change yours, too.

Don't let fear hold you captive; let fear be your compass. You are ready to change the course of your life, and you can do scary things. Facing your fears can be intimidating, and I am here for you. Send me your biggest fear, by emailing me at vitale@vitalebuford.com, and we can walk through your fear together.

I've also put together a free guide to help you face your fears. Go to www.vitalebuford.com/fearless to access my free guide, "5 Steps to go from Fearful to Fearless."

ABOUT VITALE BUFORD: *Vitale is an agent of transformation and lasting change. Aside from a professional coaching certification through iPEC and ten-plus years of corporate experience and coaching, Vitale has a superpower for helping stuck individuals take action through learning one necessary, fundamental truth: They're worth it.*

She has infused her professional education with her personal experience of overcoming a ten-year addiction and an eating disorder to create a unique coaching system. She has a very specific process she takes clients through that involves Awareness, Perspective, and Action. No two people are the same and neither are their blueprints. Each person receives a customized plan as individual as they are—based on a combination of education, experience, and intuition.

She now lives her full life with her vibrant son, snuggly lover of a dog, and a high-impact morning workout whenever possible. Discover your best life with Vitale at www.vitalebuford.com.

The Next Right Step

SHAWN HENSON

SOMETIMES, THE WAY TO navigate a difficult situation is to just "Take the next right step."

When other parents were bragging about how their children had graduated with honors, were college-bound, and had great marriages, I was just glad my daughter had not yet been arrested, didn't have an STD, and had a couch instead of sleeping in the rocks by Taco Bell... under a bush. *Mental Illness is a Bitch!*

###

The door flew open and law enforcement entered the hospital room. In one fell swoop, my daughter's boyfriend was arrested and my one-day-old granddaughter was whisked into the hallway and out of my daughter's care—forever.

There had already been problems. She had lost custody of her two older children (then aged three and seventeen months). Now, the baby was gone, too. I've often wondered if the hospital photographer was in on the plan to snatch the baby. She was in the process of taking photos and had rolled the bassinet over next to the door, as she began to take my precious granddaughter's first baby pictures. How else did the authorities know the baby would be by the door? Or did they?

It wasn't time for "I told you so." My daughter had just lost her baby, her third child that year, and was screaming in anguish, "My baby, my baby, *my baby*. Where is my baby? Where did they take my baby?!"

During her pregnancy, I had asked the social workers if they would take the baby when it was born, and they had assured me this was a separate case, a clean slate, and the baby would not be taken at the hospital. So, why did this happen? I was stunned.

While trying to take in what had just happened, my mind couldn't help but remember the words my daughter had said so often during her pregnancy: "If they take my baby, I will kill myself!" She had been suicidal in her early months of pregnancy, when she lost her other two kids, so the threat seemed real. The social worker tried to calm her, but she ran out of the hospital in her pajamas, to find out where they had taken the baby.

After she left the hospital, I found my daughter pacing in the waiting room (still in her flannel pajamas) at the Department of Children's services, hoping to talk to the agency director. Soon, we were asked to join a "meeting of the minds," to determine the next step in my daughter's child welfare case...

For twenty years, I was a supervisor in the field of social services, managing high-risk cases similar to my own daughter's. Now, as I sat at the table with the agency director, other case managers, and my daughter, I could not help but notice which side of the table I was now on. This time, I was part of "that family" at the receiving end of the "support." I felt pained by the fact that I had been able to support hundreds of other high-risk families, so they could more effectively parent their children and better their lives, yet my own daughter had refused my help.

It was during this meeting that the Children's Services director asked me, "Would you be willing to take all three children into your care? And, if you are, we will transfer the case to your county." She further added, "You would also have to find your daughter suitable housing outside of your home. Are you willing to do this?"

Without hesitation I said, "Of course." It was the right thing to do.

I had not previously been a candidate for placement of the children, because I lived outside the county where the case resided. Now, it was clear things had changed. The director agreed with my opinion that the best shot my daughter had to become mentally stable, leave her abusive boyfriend, and get her children back was to create distance from the county where he lived.

My whole life shifted. I went from being a single, almost fifty-year-old woman in the height of her career to an instant single parent of three babies. I had a newborn, a one-year-old, and a three-year-old, all of whom were in diapers and had varying special needs.

I remember my daunting schedule: commuting to a full-time job, getting kids to daycare, and, no exaggeration, over fifty appointments a month, including social workers, specialists, doctors, special education, counseling, court advocates, court-mandated visits, court hearings, and court investigation, plus driving to collect daily breast milk. I was also managing my home to the scrutiny of the social workers, the courts, and other professionals. At one point, I realized I had five home visits from five separate professionals scheduled that week! It was insane.

Those were just some of the physical demands. Emotionally, my heart was breaking as I witnessed my daughter continuing to make wrong choices. She defied the courts and secretly drove five hours to meet up with the boyfriend she had been forbidden from contacting, and then not-so-secretly posted the rendezvous publicly on social media. She lost her housing program, became homeless, and began to miss court-mandated meetings.

The house of cards began tumbling fast. Although I wanted to fully support my daughter, I had to shift my priority to protect the best interest of the kids—even if my daughter didn't like it. This meant, when I realized my daughter was smoking marijuana, I stopped giving the baby her breast milk. When she became intolerable during visits, I scaled back her contact with the kids to only court-mandated visits, supervised by social services.

Looking back, what helped me make it through this period in my life with any sense of grace and resilience was, when I didn't know what to do, I asked myself, "What's the next right step?" This was one of five factors that got me through including:

- ❖ Faith
- ❖ Support from family and friends
- ❖ Maintaining boundaries
- ❖ Self-care
- ❖ But taking the next right step was key!

Whenever I was spinning out of control with worry, anxiety, or uncertainty, I'd ask myself, "What's the next right step?"

"One day at a time" was too long, but a step was only two feet in front of me. Taking the next right step was the rudder that directed me and the propeller that kept me moving forward during this seemingly out-of-control situation.

About eleven months after I received the children, my daughter's parental rights were severed and the kids became eligible for adoption. I took the next right step: I adopted the children, and my life once again felt like my own. The social workers stopped knocking on my door, court appointments ceased, and home checks went by the wayside. We began to settle in to further solidify our little family unit.

My first big act of taking the next right step, after I adopted the kids, was to retire from my twenty-year career. I wanted to be fully available to them, to attend to their needs, and still care for myself, so I became a stay-at-home mom.

As the kids got older, I began dabbling in online business coaching. I really enjoyed interfacing as a professional with other adults, and I loved how I could create a business while having the flexibility to meet my kids' needs. What started as a bit of a hobby became a thriving business.

I realized that the five steps I'd used to overcome what seemed like an impossible situation in my personal life, actually could help to serve others. The steps are faith, support, boundaries, self-care, and "taking the next right step."

My 5-Step Framework to Success helps support my clients to keep a positive mindset and gives them the resilience needed to build their online business. These are the same assets I have relied on in my own life, when things were upside down and I didn't know exactly what to do.

Fully embracing the key to success within you can be both liberating and terrifying! It's amazing how often entrepreneurs do not recognize that things that come very easy to them are actually marketable and their greatest assets in business.

As a Clarity and Success Coach, I help entrepreneurs leverage their inherent strengths and skills to attract ideal clients and convert them to paying customers. My 5-Step

Framework to Success Principles help them take the next right steps to build their profitable business.

My 5 Step Framework to Success

1. Faith: I help my clients embrace and leverage their brilliance and tap into power (beyond what they feel they hold), in order to find the strength, resources, or perseverance they need to succeed.

2. Support: I partner with my clients and, through encouragement, gentle nudging, and offering accountability, guide them to step out in confidence and take the actions necessary to step into their success.

3. Boundaries: The key to balance, productivity, and fulfillment is all about boundaries. I help my clients identify and create boundaries, so they can enjoy their life while building a profitable business.

4. Self-Care: My clients learn to integrate self-love and taking care of their physical, emotional/social, and spiritual needs, to ensure they have the energy and stamina to thrive as a business owner.

5. Take the Next Right Step: I help my clients gain clarity and learn to trust their intuition to take the Next Right Step.

To learn more about my story, you can find me here: ShawnHenson.com/mystory.

Reach out at shawnhensoncoaching@gmail.com, and let me know if you feel stuck, overwhelmed, or unsure of your next step (in life and/or business). I am happy to send you my *Next Right Step* inspirational series, to help you move from self-doubt, distraction, lack of confidence, or overwhelm and into a state of clarity. This includes clarity of mind, spirit, and action. I look forward to hearing from you!

###

ABOUT SHAWN HENSON: *Shawn is a Clarity and Success coach who helps entrepreneurs leverage their inborn gifts, to "stand out" and create a hook that magnetizes clients. Helping women reach success, despite extreme challenges, is nothing new to Shawn. She helped high-risk women achieve life and career goals, during her 9-5 career supporting women in poverty. She now speaks domestically and internationally on the topic of "Life and Business Transformation."*

Despite her professional success helping women overcome adversity, her own adult daughter sadly would not accept her help. She lived a nightmare, as her daughter made a series of detrimental life choices leading to the loss of custody and parental rights to her children. Shawn retired from her twenty-plus-year career to adopt and be available to her youngest three children (bio-grandkids).

Single mom to four with a unique family dynamic, she is featured in the book, Amazing Moms: Parents of the 21st Century *by Dr. Elise Cohen-Ho and Hogan Hilling (Oprah-approved author). She attributes: "faith and "taking the next right step" (one of her go-to mantras) as her key to staying mentally strong when life goes topsy-*

turvy. Shawn's mantras are available in her FREE inspiration-in-60-seconds series: www.ShawnHenson.com/inspire-me. Learn more about Shawn here: www.ShawnHenson.com

The Power of Perspective

SUSANNA ESTHER KASHIEMER

IT IS ONE THING to keep one's mental game strong during the good times. It is another level of resilience when all hell is breaking loose in your life. And when you have actually planted the exact opposite seeds of the hell that seems to be manifesting in your life... *This* is yet another level of "overcome-ability," as I like to call it, that is both required and fashioned at this level of adversity.

To operate at this level with strength requires a must-have ingredient, without which the same level of inner strength is nowhere near possible. It is the Power of Perspective.

A greater perspective takes any situation that is good, bad, or otherwise and arms you with a force that lifts you beyond the circumstance. It is this powerful key that infuses the strongest of mindsets. We cannot operate from the ground-floor perspective of the mess. We must elevate and operate from the perspective of progress. Since our perspective determines our progress, we must ask ourselves, "Would I rather be sweating out my history or flowing in my destiny?"

Mastering our perspective and mindsets is a continual process of growth... and one we never "arrive" at until we are no longer on this Earth. We will always be faced with bigger challenges that help us build our mindset muscles.

My personal journey of mastering my perspective and mindset started with simply removing negative talk. I followed up with prompt action, when I feel Spirit lead, then willfully chose to align with gratitude and grace, instead of pain or offense in my heart. From there, I went on to manifest multiple thousands of dollars and then manifest the house I had written down I wanted to receive. I pursued and then had two pain-free (medication- and hypnosis-free) childbirths, using just mindset and faith. And even more beyond this.

With each consecutive "challenge," in hindsight, it's been interesting to see the hand of the Creator of the Universe showing me the playbook: ways to continually upgrade, and tips to upgrade my resilience, sharpen and broaden my perspective, and, even if it took a while, to ultimately come out winning, every single time. When you understand your purpose and then a challenge comes your way, you can zoom out to a bird's-eye view, so to speak, and gain perspective on what strategies you should employ in order to get out of the tailspin (or prevent it!) in your life and soar, instead. Let me give you an example.

June 19, 2016—Father's Day. It was a beautiful summer day and I was excited to spend the day with my family. I was nine months pregnant with my third baby and was again pursuing a pain-free childbirth using mindset and faith.

I rolled out of bed and made my way to the bathroom. Looking up in the mirror, I suddenly saw half of my face drooping and paralyzed. I found myself in the emergency room later that morning, waiting for a doctor's diagnosis. Due to the mindset work I had already been doing over my mind-body connection to prepare for a pain-free childbirth, I was feeling quite strong mentally when this paralysis hit. In hindsight, perhaps it was the grace of God, ultimately knowing what I would have to go through in its entirety.

Sitting in the waiting room that day, I felt inspired to sing the song, "It Is Well with My Soul," to bring peace to myself. As I began to sing, I fully believed there was going to be something good that came out of this situation. I knew there was no way I was doing all this faith work and mindset work only to have this random occurrence happen to my face.

The doctor finally came in and diagnosed me as having Bell's Palsy. He mentioned that, generally, it should resolve within a month or so, as is typical with that diagnosis. However, I looked far worse than the medical journal examples! Needing a customized diagnosis, I went to a neurologist a few days later.

Having been a professional singer, actress, model, vocal coach, and life coach, I knew my face was important to my career. Knowing that, as a voice and a communicator, not being able to speak clearly or even meet my lips together to sing anymore was *not* okay for me. These things were part of my destiny and my gifts, with which I serve the world, so no way I was going to let this take up residence in my body! It simply was a non-negotiable.

So, when I headed to the neurologist's office that day, I had already decided I was not going to get depressed or discouraged by whatever his report was. As the expert in his field, I was going to him simply to get the parameters of what I was facing, so I could have quantifiable measures of how to know *when* I was getting better, because I *knew* I would. Knowing my calling and purpose helped ground me in this perspective.

It may be helpful to note here that there is a typical grading scale doctors use to determine the severity of Bell's Palsy, called the House-Brackmann Facial Nerve Grading System. Grade 1 would be normal function, while the highest grade given is Grade 6, which is complete and total paralysis. So, as it stands, the lower the grade of severity, the better the prognosis for recovery.

Based on the findings recorded in the US National Library of Medicine at the National Institute of Health, as well as the Facial Paralysis Institute, typically, the average patient with Bell's Palsy falls in the Grade 2-3 range. Ninety-four percent of these folks recover fully, and about eighty to eight-five percent recover within three months or less, mostly within thirty days. After numerous tests, my neurologist determined what I had was a Grade 5, severe case of Bell's Palsy, with complete to near complete paralysis. His prognosis, based on my tests, determined that eighty percent of my facial nerves had been damaged. He said, *if* I recovered, it would likely take nine to eighteen months to see some recovery, and even then, only a fifty- to sixty-percent chance of recovery at that. I let the information sink in and thanked him for his expertise then went home and made a plan.

Knowing that we are integrated beings made of mind, body, soul, and spirit, I knew my healing and full recovery would indeed come from addressing my whole being holistically. To address my body, I researched and took foods to decrease inflammation of that nerve and boosted nerve-healthy foods, essential oils, and massages. For the soul, I attuned my heart to see if there was anyone I was holding unforgiveness to and released forgiveness. Our bodies hold trauma, and it has been proven that emotions, negative or positive, have an effect on our mind-body connection, as well. Having cleared any of these negative, toxic things from my soul, I additionally deposited hope into and nourished my soul by what I surrounded myself with in regards to inspiring podcasts and transformative music.

As for the mind, I visualized my face completely healed, which was no easy feat. Standing in front of the mirror, I saw looking back at me a drooping, paralyzed face with little chance of full recovery. I had to decisively choose to replace the logical report of my chances of recovery and to partner with a higher perspective of the situation, downloading that new picture of my outcome into my mind and heart, and then bringing that perspective into my present....

I did this daily, multiple times a day. I visualized myself on videos, stages, books, podcasts, and other forms of media, sharing the story of my healing and recovery and continuing to fulfill my calling, despite this setback. From this new belief,

I began to activate resurrection power over the deadened nerves and commanded the inflammation to leave and the nerves to regenerate, while I envisioned them doing so. This is where I believe the mind instructs the rest of our being to follow suit. What we believe, we see. What we see, we create.

Spiritually, I sang songs to myself that realigned my focus on faith versus fear and filled me with possibilities, instead of negativity and doubt. My spirit and soul in tandem were electing to see this setback instead as a set*up* for greater possibilities I hadn't envisioned before. Additionally, the pure synergy of several friends, family, and even people whom I had never met before, all over the world, praying for my recovery, intensified the reality of this outcome from just a figment of my imagination into tangible reality. I continually charged up my spirit with powerful words of life, inspiration, purpose, and perspectives of possibilities. This was my fuel to pour into my mind, body, and soul from this overflow, and because I was intimate with my purpose, I was consistent with it.

Three months later, I went in for a follow-up with my neurologist. He redid all the tests and, with quiet puzzlement, went back and forth, doing double takes between his computer notes and my face! Finally, he looked at me quizzically and said, "You have recovered more than most people that come through here, and you had quite the severe case! What happened?"

I thanked him and said, "I believe we are not just body but mind, soul, and spirit, as well. I knew, if I wanted my whole 'vehicle' to go in the direction of healing, I needed to address all four 'tires,' not just one." I then shared with him what I'd done.

Still looking at me intently, he said, "You are aware of this stuff more than the average person."

I shrugged my shoulders and told him, "These possibilities and dimensions exist, whether we all are aware of them or not, so we might as well be aware and activate them!"

He wrote his follow-up report, which stated, "She *had* Bell's Palsy back in June. I'm happy to report she has had excellent improvement. Vastly improved Bell's Palsy. Nerves have regenerated."

To this day, I continue to enjoy the ninety-percent recovery that was never promised me and continue to pursue even greater and more complete recovery, which I believe will continue to happen as I encourage others with my story, because I believe this didn't just happen *to* me, but *for* me and *through* me, to be an encouragement to *you*. How can I do this? Having the right *perspective* on my purpose. I've learned (and continue to learn) <u>not</u> to ask, "Why is this happening *to* me?" But rather, "How is this happening *for* me? What am I here to learn... and then give?" And then, I go after it 100%, like it has my name on it. This is critical.

Without learning from our challenges, we drastically stunt our own growth. Without activating our mindset and faith, we are actually deteriorating inside.

Understanding the power of perspective arms us to win, no matter what, *every single time.* The truth is, hidden within what you've been through is your breakthrough. Successively, within your breakthrough is your authority to release breakthroughs for others. Nothing is ever wasted..., unless you get stuck only seeing what you've been through.

We must remember that it is not for our own personal benefit alone that we pursue greater perspective. It is for *the rising.* The rising of ourselves, yes. But also for the ability to then—with that newfound authority—graciously invite others, including our families, community, nation, and world, into that rising, as well. It is in the rising that our truest selves are uncovered. Who we are meant to be is revealed in **adversity**, in the **fire**, in the **storm**. Therein lies the opportunity to release and shake off the toxic buildup of sludge put on us by others and, most often, by ourselves. The storm serves to *be* the shaking, the fire serves to *burn* off the sludge. The adversity serves to *turn* us into who we are created to be.

Even the word *adversity* hints to us the potential hiding within it. Using Latin definitions:

"AD" - "toward," "with regard to"

"VERS" - "turned," "turning"

"ITY" - "Condition or quality of being"

So, in essence, the nature and purpose of adversity is *with regard to* or *toward* a *turning* and *condition or quality of being turned*.

Did you catch that?

The hidden purpose of adversity is to present to you the opportunity to turn/transform. I would add to turn/rise or transform into a greater expression of yourself and of Divine Presence that seeks to partner with and emanate through you.

But... what if you never saw it as such? Which part of your brilliant true self would our world never have the honor of knowing? What solutions would that developed and honed true self not ever bring to your life, your family, and our world, because we would rather deny ourselves the fight..., when we are already the victor?

We all can attest to the fact that part of the human experience is going through highs and lows. Unfortunately, most of us are seemingly programmed to have the perspective that we should maximize our time, pursuing the highs and minimizing or avoiding the lows. But who could we become, if we understood a different perspective?

What if we saw it is in the lows that we are able to evolve into a greater expression of ourselves or mature into a higher version of our true self? How are we holding ourselves back, our families back, or our world back from rising because we are not *employing* our numerous adversities with an upgraded perspective? Each and every one of us has messes in our lives. But those of us who take the messes, stop blaming everyone else, and Activate Greatness in our own lives emerge powerfully with a *message*.

MESSES + A‌ctivating G‌reatness = **MESSAGES.**

You may be only a couple letters away from transforming your messes into messages! It's time to upgrade!

While the most painful situations seem like huge setbacks, when surrendered, they transform into *setups*..., just the catalyst we needed all along to launch us into the next level of our growth and expansion. This is the gift that a greater perspective grants us. Knowing our purpose activates that greatness hidden inside each of us, so our mind, soul, body, and spirit has the fortitude to actually contain that freedom we all deeply desire. That is my hope for you and me!

If this resonates with you, I'd love to hear from you! If you are struggling with grabbing ahold of perspectives that flip the script and create more winning outcomes in your life, if you are wanting to be clear and unshakeable in your purpose, and if you are craving strategies that will cause fear, doubt, and shame to no longer have a hold on you but actually fear *you*, instead, then contact me at susannaesthercoach@gmail.com.

I will send to you my free 5-step guide as my gift for reading this book! Whatever situations you are dealing with that may require an upgraded perspective, you will gain insight and activations in my 5-step guide, showing you step-by-step how to transform Fear to Freedom! Download the free guide, do the steps, and do let me know how it is helping you in your life! You can also connect with me over at www.susannaesther.com.

Let's collaborate in upgrading your perspective and living in alignment with your amazing purpose. Our world needs more resilient, out-of-the-box, brilliant, creative, soulful women living out our purpose with freedom! I can't wait to connect with you!

###

ABOUT SUSANNA ESTHER KASHIEMER: *Susanna is lit up by seeing people transform their pain and limited thinking to shifting mindsets and living out their greatest destiny! Her mission in life is to be a voice and light, communicating truths from a unique perspective that results in this transformative freedom.*

Susanna is a Freedom Life Coach and Mindset maven, spirit/soul seer, musician, speaker and writer. Having studied personal development, spirituality, inner healing, and purpose for decades, she also has added degrees in vocal performance and communication, media, and psychology. Her background is lush with creative performance—as a professional singer, vocal coach, actress, and model. Beyond all this, she is most passionate about the work of uniting mind, body, soul and spirit and bringing healing of the true self.

She is called to make an impact through media (books, music, film, social media, and more) to upgrade the consciousness of those who are ready to wake up, shine, and change the world through the transformative change they experience within!

Her most amazing work unfolds daily in three little handsome world-changers, who are her delight! She can be found somewhere between having dance parties in her house of high-octane boys, depositing life-grounding truths for them in lots of heart-to-hearts, or connecting with other creative, soulful, powerful women in person and through her website at www.susannaesther.com.

When Life Gives You Lemons, Add Limes and Make Margaritas!

SARA KIRSCH

1996 WAS THE YEAR that changed my life.

No, change is the wrong word.

Devastated is more appropriate.

It was the senior year of high school for me. I was doing all sorts of things in and outside of school.

I was a leader in band, student conductor for my chambers choral group, student conductor for Pinellas Youth Symphony, Lieutenant Governor for Key Club, active in so many school clubs, and volunteering outside of school.

I was getting decent grades and making my parents and grandparents proud.

I had huge plans to go to a major music school, like Eastman School of Music or Juilliard, so I could get my degree in music performance.

I had the next five to ten years of my life laid out.

I had the drive. I had the ambition. And I had it all planned out.

Until that day in December 1996.

Three days before my eighteenth birthday, my parents surprised me with a mini-trip from Tampa Bay to Pensacola, as part of my birthday present.

Single-engine flying lessons.

I had expressed an interest for years in getting my private pilot's license, and we had a family friend who was a flight instructor. I had done my own studying of the mechanicals and requirements, prepping for the day when I could finally take lessons up in the air.

So, on December 27, 1996, my parents made the decision to make my dream come true. I was going to get my first flying lesson, while we took a short day-trip to Pensacola to visit some family and friends. We would leave early the next day for our adventure.

The morning of December 28 was clear and cold, but our pilot wasn't worried. He'd flown thousands of hours, and many of them in the exact plane we were flying in.

I was terrified and excited all at once. I sat right next to him in the co-pilot position, while my parents sat in the back. The plane was a six-seater, so they had plenty of room to stretch out and enjoy the ride.

Little did I know this flight would change my life forever.

The flight itself was both exhilarating and terrifying. I sat there, amazed, as we lifted off from the runway and climbed through the clouds. As we flew along the west Florida coast, I even got to see the tops of the Crystal River power plant towers—something I had only seen from the ground.

I had flown before, but only commercially, never in a single-engine plane.

Everything was going smoothly until we arrived in foggy Pensacola.

That's when the engine stopped and our pilot couldn't restart it.

We fell from the sky, from 2000 feet. A very surreal moment, let me tell you.

You know those Bugs Bunny cartoons where the plane goes nose down and then stops right before it hits the ground? It was almost like watching that cartoon in super-slow motion from *inside* the plane, except we didn't stop. I watched as the wing next to me was ripped away when we hit the first trees, then the plane flipping as the tail caught some others.

Then, nothing but eerie silence. Nothing.

Emergency personnel eventually reached us, a hundred feet off the road, after traversing through mud and sewage. My mom had been thrown from the plane and died instantly. My dad was able to get out of the wreckage, although he doesn't remember anything of what happened. The pilot was buried three feet in the ground next to me. And I was trapped under the plane, held in by my seat belt.

They eventually got me out, and I spent four days in the hospital (including my eighteenth birthday), with major head trauma and needing reconstructive surgery on my head and face. I didn't have any broken bones and was lucky to be alive.

Here it is, twenty-one years later, and I still have nightmares *every night* about the crash: a video playback of everything that happened.

But it changed everything for me. I was told by several different neurologists that, if I continued to play my bassoon and oboe professionally, there was a twenty-times greater chance I would die of an aneurysm. So, music performance was now off the table as a career.

I felt lost. Utterly and completely lost. What now?

I didn't know what else I could do. I had been preparing for the past five years for a career performing in orchestras, and now that dream had been snatched away from me.

In an instant.

Fall 1997 was when I was supposed to go to college, but instead of going to Eastman or Juilliard, I ended up at USF. I thought that trying to go back to a normal life would be best, but it didn't work out. Mistake #1. After one semester, I withdrew from USF and started going to my local community college, while working two jobs, trying to figure out the next steps.

Summer 1998, I married my high school sweetheart. Mistake #2.

In 1999, my dad remarried. To the pilot's widow. I supported his decision, despite the rest of the family's disapproving. Mistake #3.

In 1999 and 2001, I welcomed two great little boys.

In 2003, my husband and I separated, and then we divorced in 2004. Great decision #1. It was an abusive relationship that my family knew nothing about, not that they were willing to listen to me, anyway. They had been lied to by my ex while I remained silent, hoping we could resolve our issues between us. But my "family" wasn't even willing to listen to me by the time I broke down and asked for help.

So, I stopped talking to them, basically cutting them out of my life. Great decision #2.

That's when I really started getting serious about my side hustles. Great decision #3.

Even though I was now a divorced mom to two boys, I worked a job and ran a business to support myself, especially since my ex-husband was a real jerk and wouldn't support his own kids.

I had always had a side hustle, ever since graduating high school. My first business was running a custom computer consultancy. It broke even and was great for tax purposes. My second business was a graphic design business that was sort of profitable, but not wildly.

The third business was a photography business—mostly weddings, but commercial work, too. I started doing really well there, until all my commercial clients started to ask for other things, like marketing, social media, and design. All of that took up a lot of my time.

I was really good at both, but I had to make the choice: photography or marketing.

I chose *marketing*. This is what I've been doing ever since.

And I LOVE it!

I'll be honest, though. It's not all unicorns and instant manifestations of what I want. Since that fateful day in 1996, I've had to come up with a new plan—a new purpose. And that hasn't been easy.

In 2012, I got together with a fabulous guy named Fritz, and things really started changing for the better. But it wasn't until 2015 that I got super-clear about what I wanted to do, where I wanted to go with my business, and what I wanted to do in life. Until then, I had only "survived."

Even now, there are some really hard days. Especially when I feel like I'm not supported by anyone. No family (except my hubby and kids), few friends. Many of my friends work regular jobs, so they don't understand what the stresses and unique issues I face, as an entrepreneur and small-business owner. But I don't let it faze me, thanks to a little piece of advice I've held on to for years now.

Let me rewind back to 1997 for a moment.

Since I was a Lt. Governor for Key Club, I had to attend the Annual Key Club conference. While I was there (Spring '97), I had the opportunity to have breakfast with the then-Governor of Kiwanis. His name was Vann Banks, and he told me something that morning that I've carried with me all these years, through everything I've experienced. It has warded off depression, kept me trying new things, and is my lifeline, when I feel alone in the world.

"If it is to be, it is up to me."

Ten two-letter words that changed my life.

Vann told me I am the creator of my destiny. And that everyone on this Earth is here for a reason. But it was up to me to find it and share that purpose and my talents. If I didn't, I would be denying a portion of the world the opportunity to learn and grow from whatever I could teach.

Because, we're all teachers, in some way or form. Maybe it's just showing someone how to get better at hitting a baseball. Or perfecting their dance routine. Or getting organized in their business, so they can be profitable and give back to the local community.

It only takes one person to make a difference. And the difference doesn't have to be huge. Even the smallest effort makes ripples across time and space and multiplies, as it goes away from the center, creating wave after wave of effects. Watch something fall into water and you'll see that ripple effect. Same concept, except you stay dry.

Every person who is reading this book has something to teach. To give. And if you don't, you're denying the world your passion, your talents, your purpose.

And no matter what stage in life you're at, there's always an opportunity. I could have easily given up in 1996-97. Instead, I chose to find something new. It was a choice I would make time and again, no matter what life has thrown at me. And believe me, there's been quite a few times I felt like giving in.

So, let me teach you something, as small as it is. No matter where you are in your business or your life, there is opportunity. So, seize it. With both hands and *don't let go!*

You *are* worth it. And don't let anyone tell you that you aren't. Those are not your friends.

This is what I've dedicated my business and my life to: helping people find their purpose, their passion, and then *do* something with it.

Helping them find peace of mind, knowing their family is covered. Knowing they're doing business right, while reaching their goals. Helping them make their side hustles into real businesses that make a profit on *their* terms. And more.

So, if you want to make a difference in your own life or someone else's—No Matter Where You've Been—you have to start by making a choice.

You have to choose *yourself*. There's a reason why the airlines always announce for you to put your own oxygen mask on first, before you help anyone else. Because you cannot help others if you don't help stabilize yourself first.

Let me help you create the life and/or business you've always wanted. No matter how alone you think you are, you already have someone on your side who *does* understand.

Me.

And here's my pledge to you:

"I, Sara Kirsch, promise to help you find your calling in life and always be a cheerleader on your side. I promise to help you in any way I can and help you succeed with all the tools at my disposal. All I ask is that you show up and try. Try your damnedest and be willing to try something new. And I'll be right beside you for as long as you need me."

It's time. It's *your* time. Let's take that first step together, because you are *not* alone.

Let's get this dream going. Together.

Because *If It Is To Be, It Is Up To YOU*.

And here's a present for you, because the *present* is the time to start your journey. Go to my website (listed below) and get your free gift.

Why am I doing this? Because I love to help people start their own journeys of freedom, joy, and happiness. And I want to see you succeed. I want to help you overcome doubt, fear, and helplessness.

And you shouldn't have to do it alone. Because building *anything* takes more than one person, and you already have one person on your side—me.

Go to: MarketingIsNotSelling.com/MasterYourInnerGameBook/

ABOUT SARA KIRSCH: *Sara is an expert in marketing, accounting and all things business. She is a mom of two boys and has owned a business in one form or another for the past twenty years, helping her clients generate well over $40 million in sales while increasing their profits and covering their assets. Sara has worked with small-business owners in just about every industry and from around the world, assisting them to find the right customers and fall in love with their businesses again.*

Her business is Marketing Is Not Selling—debunking business myths that hold people back from achieving true success and financial freedom while living life authentically and passionately, teaching through e-courses, group programs, business coaching, and custom-tailored strategy plans.

website: www.MarketingIsNotSelling.com

Free Gift: *"Taking Your First Steps Towards Freedom—a 5-day mini-challenge to help you jumpstart your dreams NOW!"* Find it here: *www.MarketingIsNotSelling.com/MasterYourInnerGameBook/*

A Dreamer, A Believer, and an Achiever in Transformation

CHRISTY LITTLE

I HAD HIT A WALL. I saw it happening, but I just couldn't stop.

My career as a professional dancer was going from thriving to collapsing right underneath me. The injuries kept coming, fatigue was setting in, and my spirit was dwindling, all within a matter of months. I'm not sure what happened, what switch flipped off inside me, but the path I was on propelled me far off track.

I hung up my dancin' shoes. It was such a strange decision, abruptly taken around negative energy. I didn't even try to find a solution; I simply gave up. The black cloud that hung over my head was large and in charge. It followed me everywhere, forever reminding me my life had become unidentifiable.

Now, as a dancer, I'd always understood that our retirement age is significantly younger than most career paths and this moment in life was inevitable. Yet, I was not prepared for it to arrive in my twenties. I had no other plan and didn't know any other way to make money.

What once was a life full of excitement, travel, and new opportunities became a sluggish existence, where I just fumbled along, trying to find my new place. I wanted to be a good financial partner for my husband, but I also wanted to keep my passions alive. Neither of those things were happening. My feelings of failure were overwhelming. That's when I became constantly anxious and mentally self-sabotaging.

Everything at that time made me feel like I was drowning. Any of the self-confidence I had gained through performing was zapped out of me. My perspective became totally driven by my inner mean girl, who told me I now sucked. The anxiety that had been present for most of my life grew so strong that, many days, I was made physically ill. My mind had spun out of control and I felt totally helpless to the noise.

This went on until I couldn't take it anymore. The burning desire to live a life that truly called to me wouldn't quit. Finally, I got out of my own way and listened.

Some tiny voice made its way to the surface, above all the mental chatter, and asked that I open my mind. I had come across a Lao Tzu quote that resonated with me so greatly, it snapped me out of my funk: "If you are depressed, you are living in the past. If you are anxious, you are living in the future. If you are at peace, you are living in the present."

LIGHTBULB! You can only live in the present moment... The rest doesn't exist! It quite literally is not reality.

I became aware that I can control how I react to the thoughts that enter my mind. I had always been worrying about the "what ifs?" and the "how will I evers?" and pretty much none of those concerns ever even happened to me. It was a huge waste of time and ruined any chance of enjoying my present moments—you know, the ones I could actually control. At this point, I began conditioning my mind with as much care as I did my body.

Meditation was something I had been totally resistant to. I played up a good talk in my head about why it wasn't for me: I couldn't quiet my thoughts and believed there was nothing I could do about it. But my point of desperation was so deep, I knew in my gut I had to open my mind.

The process was far from peaceful, in the beginning. My sessions lasted about ten seconds before thoughts came flooding back in. However, I allowed myself grace through this time, knowing it was going to take practice. With a heightened awareness, I was able to acknowledge when my mind focused on my "fake" reality and then could quiet the noise. I began to look for any opportunity to stop my thoughts for as long as I could: while idling at a red light, waiting in a check-out line, brushing my teeth—basically any time I could find. It was just like all the other physical conditioning exercises I did—I had to build the technique.

With this new enlightenment, I learned other ways of staying centered. A peaceful demeanor became the daily goal. I practiced gratitude, focusing on all the great aspects of my life each night, before I went to sleep. When I could recognize these things, my energy toward each day changed and brought me more wonderful moments.

I realized it's a waste to focus on all the negative, because all that does is keep you in a state of "ugh." This was not going to bring me the fabulous life I desired. I began to look for answers on the inside, instead of looking for external solutions. The more often I sat quietly with myself, the easier it was to find my answers and my direction. This changed everything for me. In doing so, what came next was pretty fabulous.

At this point, I had little natural energy; I was so tired all the time. My travel coffee cup became my obsessive companion, what got me through each day. I had been working hard to find physical solutions to get my dancer's body back, but I just didn't seem to have any oomph to me. My diet had always been healthy and pretty strict, so I never gave it any thought as to whether I was lacking nutrients. But I was particularly open-minded one day when I stumbled onto something.

I started using a nutritional system that I'd hoped would help me get back my old stamina. Optimistic that this would youthfully rejuvenate me, I took a chance on something without a guarantee, because it felt right in my gut. With my improved mindset, it was clear that what I had tried so far wasn't enough to get me dancing fulltime again, so taking this chance was a good option.

Within days of having this nutrition, I felt completely different. Every cell in my body felt awake. My energy came back. I was sleeping better. This enabled me to condition more intensely than I had in years, which in turn gave me even more to put into my gratitude practice. Seeing the glimmer of hope that this nutrition might revive my career sent me into massive action. I filled hours of my day with workouts, ballet classes, meditation, and reading books on enlightenment. I was on a mission to change the trajectory of my current path.

The evolution of this physical and spiritual exploration restored everything for me. I have been able to return to the stage with a strong, able body and a peaceful mind. With this nutrition, I have regained my natural energy, stamina, and motivation. With my newfound inner connection, I no longer am pained with panic attacks or anxiety. Life is so fulfilling now, it has me springing out of bed each morning. As a result, my husband and I have moved across the country to be exposed to more growth opportunities. We embrace getting uncomfortable now, because we know that leads to greatness.

In addition to my renewed dance career, I have jumped on an opportunity to have my own business sharing the nutritional knowledge I've gained. In this pursuit, I am helping people physically free themselves, showing them what a limitless mindset can do for their lives. I encourage people to dream again. Each energized day is so thrilling for me now.

This journey has truly shown me we all can accomplish anything we set our minds on and a healthy body also includes a healthy mind. You are what you feed yourself—both in your thoughts as well as in your body. Whatever feels aligned with your true self is what you deserve. It is my mission to show people what's possible in themselves.

I'm a dreamer, a believer, and an achiever in transformation. Living that motto each day, I intend to share this vision with all those who are courageous enough to open their minds.

I invite you to dream with me. Please send me an email at thedancingoptimist@gmail.com, and I will send you my free guide: *Daily Practices for a Flourishing Body and Mind*. These are the essential game-changers I've implemented in my everyday life, and I'd love to share them with you.

###

ABOUT CHRISTY LITTLE: *Christy is a professional dancer and wellness mentor. Her career has given her the opportunity to perform nationally and internationally in many facets, allowing travel to become one of her favorite indulgences. She has spent over a decade aligned in her true spirit on stages, directing, choreographing, teaching, and aiming to be a positive light for all who dream.*

In addition to her creative side, Christy now is integrating in her roster her insights in the health and wellness field. She aims to educate others on the power of both mindset and the physical and mental benefits of proper nutrition. Christy believes optimal health must include a well mind, not just a well body, and they must go hand in hand. Overcoming a life of anxiety and severe panic attacks allowed her to come to this realization, which she now wants to be an example of. While guiding individuals to find their best nutritional solutions, she also wants to be an example of what inner peace can bring to one's life. To learn more about Christy, her story, and what she can offer, visit thedancingoptimist.com.

I Am In Control Over Myself

ROSEANNEY LIU

IN LIFE, THERE ARE three types of people on the spectrum:

- Those who want to and will help you
- Those who want to knock you off your game because they've got issues
- Those who don't care either way

What remains a constant with regard to all these groups of people you come across is *YOU.* You still dictate the terms of how hard you work on your game, how you choose to react to situations and others' responses, and how you deal with circumstances that do not define you.

When I was nine my parents divorced. My conservative, frugal mother had finally had it with my mostly absent father, who'd gambled away part of their joint savings. Despite growing up severely hard of hearing and stigmatized by society simply because she was female and deemed not as important as the male heirs in the family, my mother had fought for and kept her economic stability and independence.

She wasn't about to let my father's philandering ways compromise our life further. It's fair to say my mom was my first role model in that she did not let circumstances define who she was as a young woman and was not ever going to play the victim.

In the late '80s in Taiwan, being raised by divorced parents was kind of a big deal. As a well-liked student placing in the top ten percent of my class, year after year for the first five years, I suddenly did not know how to deal with sympathetic or surprised looks from classmates when I'd drop the D-word and mention that my dad was not living with my mom anymore. I was the only one in my class who had divorced parents. *"What?! Why?!"* was the common response from my third-grade friends, when I'd say my dad did not live with us anymore. For the first time, I understood what shame felt like.

I did not know then that more surprises and situations that would make me grow thick skin fast were just around the corner.

At age nine, I understood clearly for the first time that others' compliments of my academic achievements helped drive me to keep on achieving, because I wanted the recognition; and that, just as much, others' pity or negative reactions about my family life created a certain reaction within me. I did not know then I am in charge of my own feelings and reactions to other people's responses to what happens to me, good or bad. But I know it now.

For a long time, I learned to brush away my classmates' scrutiny over my parents' divorce by changing the subject or lying, saying, "Oh, it's okay. I feel fine about it." I did not know how to tell the truth—that the divorce hurt, that being labeled as a broken family hurt, that friends' looks of pity or sympathy hurt. And I did not know how to own my feelings and not let others' opinions dictate my opinion of myself.

I continued to work hard in school and remain as a top student, because it was the one area I had complete control over. I had to keep the academic life "perfect," since my family life was not, anymore. When my mother told me we were moving to California for good, during the fall semester of fifth grade, I had only a month to get my bearings after the visa approval and prepare for what was going to be loss of friends, of language, and of belonging to everything I had known for the first eleven years of my life. I had no idea how hard it was going to be as an outsider and how to deal with racism for the first time.

Just like I brushed away the topic of my parents' divorce in Taipei, in my new elementary school in California, I tried to pretend everything was fine and that I'd fit in. I mumbled through the Pledge of Allegiance on day one, like I knew what in the world I was saying, while my big buddy—a same-aged Japanese-American girl—watched me quizzically. I tried using the few American English phrases I had learned the summer before in Taipei and felt immediate embarrassment when I could see classmates did not understand me, probably because of my initial accent or simply due to my not using the conversational phrases correctly. I felt shame all over again, this time even more pronounced, as I knew I was the one producing the awful things that made me embarrassed.

But I soldiered on. Feeling like polite guests all the time in my aunt's home, which was my new home, my mother and I did our best to be good guests and still be comfortable, while sharing a tiny room. However, you only feel only so comfortable in someone else's home.

I attended English as a Second Language lessons with a teacher aide, Mrs. O' Kelly—one of the first in the group of people who could and wanted to help me (those I mentioned in the beginning of the chapter). She came to my new classroom every day; I also went to circle time every other day with students five years younger than I, in a classroom behind mine, to learn vocabulary and be part of Q&A for the story the teacher read to the six-year-olds. Putting on display my language learning awkwardness, accent, and mistakes was my new academic life and lasted for a year, when I was eleven.

During that time, I missed terribly my old life as a top student. I had to learn to become stronger while putting my vulnerabilities out there in order to learn the dominant language. I even had to learn the new classroom culture that was desired in American society, something not nearly as prominent in Taiwanese schools—that to be considered a good student, I had to *show* what I knew, which entailed a lot of hand-raising, group work, and being outspoken enough to call out classmates and even teachers, when they'd make mistakes.

My eleven-year-old self learned that the school-life game had changed drastically and there were now new rules I had to apply, to survive. It was incumbent upon me to learn as quickly as I could, because the nice teachers and classmates could only carry me so far.

And, at some points, I would encounter not-so-nice classmates.

Taiwan was, and still is, a homogeneous country: everyone speaks one of two dominant languages, everyone has dark hair, and, for the most part, Taiwanese people are very warm and helpful to strangers, local and visitors alike. But we all know Los Angeles is a melting pot, and, as such, racial and cultural tensions break out in different ways and to varying degrees.

My first brush with racism was when a female classmate in my fifth-grade class pulled my hair from behind me, pulled my backpack down while I was wearing it, and when I turned around to confront her, taunted, "Why don't you open your eyes, China? Open your eyes!" while her friend next to her snickered.

I understood right then this wasn't just your run-of-the-mill prankish thing happening between classmates. My race and cultural background were considered inferior to hers, and she wanted me to know that's what she thought. I wasn't mentally or emotionally equipped to deal with this racially charged confrontation, so I ignored her as much as I could, since it was near the end of the school day.

I ran home and cried my eyes out to my mother, retelling the story to my aunt and uncle when they came home that night from work. That classmate is part of the second group of people I mentioned in the beginning: the group that wants to take you off your game, because they've got issues within themselves they haven't dealt with.

A talk among my aunt, uncle, and teacher the next day kept some distance between that classmate and me for a while. So, my tears dried, we kept away from each other, and I moved on.

As a young adult and especially as a working adult raising kids of my own now, I learned there will always be critics—racist or not—in my life, like in everyone's life. Critics are as sure a thing as death and taxes. There will be good ones who give you constructive feedback (e.g., my book marketing author mentors), and there will be bad ones who simply don't like you for whatever reasons. Although I felt a lot of confusion and emotional upset over that incident in fifth grade, and there have been plenty of racist incidents since, overt and subtle—where someone would not like me because of my skin color or my eye shape or where I came from—I've had to be strong for myself, despite anyone's opinions of me.

There will be people who love my books and the talks I give for my audience, and there will be people who hate me or my stuff. There will be people who love that I hike so much and have a thirst for outdoor adventures, and there will be people who criticize me for taking some time away from family to do the things I love, or who think I was naïve to attempt hiking on Kilimanjaro with only six months' hiking experience.

One thing is for certain, though: I have to be me and live for me and not for others' opinions or the stigmas they try to put against me, because they are really none of my business. I learned that my circumstances do not define me and that some can, in fact, make me stronger and better. I learned that throughout it all, I can and must exercise control over my own actions and reactions, because everyone and everything else is a variable that is beyond my control.

If you, too, want to start living as the confident boss of your life, download my complimentary tips on how to do that, starting today. Please visit my website www.Roseanney.com and scroll to the bottom, drop your email, and download that freebie today. Your own badassery—that inner confidence over which you have complete control—is just around the corner. My book, *Badassery 101,* which covers ten secrets or ways to harness your confidence, is also available on Amazon.

###

ABOUT ROSEANNEY LIU: *Roseanney is the best-selling author behind* You Did WHAT Now?! *(2017) and* How to Survive Elementary School

(2017). Her third book, Badassery 101: Ten Secrets to Be the Confident Boss of Your Life, *was released August 2018. Besides fourteen years of English-language teaching experience to foreign students, she is also a speaker about self-confidence, networking, and independent publishing, and she helps teach the college market and associations how to show up to pursue goals with method, resourcefulness, and passion. She's been featured in* Our South Bay magazine, Readers' Favorite, *plus on numerous podcasts such as* Parent Pump Radio, A Lott of Help, *and* It's Talk Time. *An avid mountain hiker and traveler, Roseanney lives in Redondo Beach, California with her family.*

Website: www.Roseanney.com
FB: Write on, Roseanney
Intagram:roseanneyliu

Take Your Power Back for Success

JEN RYAN

IT HAD BEEN A WEEK of preparing. I had planned myself a jam-packed stretch of days that started with a close friend's wedding and would end with me at a lake house in New York for my annual trip with dear old friends.

Okay, heels? Check. Bathing suit? Check. Dress, shampoo, mascara... My mental list was then interrupted by an unexpected phone call I had no time carved out to take.

Main Office flashed on the screen. I racked my brain for any reason they could have for calling me right before the start of our long Labor Day weekend, but I told myself to take care of whatever they needed now, so I could go on to enjoy the next week.

"Hello," I answered as I zipped up my suitcase, phone sandwiched between ear and shoulder.

"Hey, Jen, we're sorry to say we are taking our business in a different direction, and your position has been eliminated."

It was like I'd been struck by lightning. *Why is this happening now?* I didn't have the time to process it. I was headed to my friend's wedding, which was supposed to be her happiest of days, so I decided to compartmentalize and press on as normal.

Over the next six days, I hid my news from friends and family. I carried it like some secret shame and still put on the smile, made the jokes, and tried to seem like my normal self. I replied to the common question, "How's work?" with a dismissive, "Everything's fine." Even at the lake house, among my closest friends, I couldn't tell anyone. Perhaps it was my pride. I didn't want the pity party or to be the center of attention with my sad tale of misfortune. Or perhaps not telling anyone made the situation less real, less permanent.

Whether or not I showed it, the truth was I was paralyzed. The fear overtook me in some moments. That phone call had left me with a kind of whiplash. How could I have let this force outside of myself hold my future hostage, just so it could be ripped away from me on a whim? I was defeated. Powerless. Embarrassed at my failure, as if there was anything I could have done to prevent it. And there wasn't enough alcohol in the state of New York to numb every overwhelming feeling that consumed me.

Fast-forward to me home again. On to "normal life."

My first day back, I took Lulu, my German shepherd, to the beach to walk and to hear the calming sound of the ocean, which hopefully would clear some of the stress that had been building up in my brain over the past week. I listened to the ocean roll itself onto the shore, as it has always done, true to its purpose. I watched the push and pull of water. A perfectly timed dance. I wondered how it could do it, so sure and fearless, each day. No questions. No insecurity. Just assured movement.

I could feel my own fear bubbling up again. I thought about my bills, my mortgage, car payment, groceries. Worries and concerned voices flooded my head. *Résumé, interviews, job, money.* What did all this mean for me? What was I going to make of it?

Despite the fear, defeat, and anxiety of the unknown that I was going to have to face, I knew I had to start with being honest with myself. Because, in that moment, all I had was me. I had to become my own advocate.

The truth was my job had been unfulfilling for a long time, and yet, somehow, I had let it become my entire identity. I didn't know who I was without it. It had become my purpose. I realized I needed to rediscover myself, if I was going to be able to move forward and find any kind of new success. For years, I realized, I had been living a lie. It was a lie that had stretched over the past decade of my life.

I thought back to when I had first moved back to New England, just before getting my corporate job. I came to New Hampshire after ending a dead-end relationship for which I had, a year prior, sold my own business. I gave far too much of myself. Hearing the waves crash, I remembered sitting in that empty apartment in a city I knew nothing about, my life boxed up and relocated and also somehow redefined. But, really, undefined. The truth was, as I sat there, I had no idea who I was. I had been drowning in the wake of a decision that had completely derailed me. My identity was broken, and so I'd made a choice to take a job that allowed me to take on someone else's identity, rather than mend my own.

One thing I was sure of, though, was I would never hear those paralyzing words again. I would never again give someone else the upper hand over my life, my job, or my happiness. I wouldn't let someone else hold my fate. My destiny. My power. I would own my future, win or lose, and it would be on my terms. Not in the direction that someone else was taking their business.

So, how was this self-discovery going to happen? Or, better yet, how was I going to make it happen and take my life back? I knew I would have to look inward.

And so, I decided to get on my yoga mat. I needed a space where I felt safe enough to let go of all the worry. To let go of everything I so desperately wanted to control but couldn't. The only thing I could control was myself. My intention.

I breathed. I connected myself not to the past, but to the present moment, and in doing so began to slowly see more clearly exactly where I was. Those honest moments with myself cultivated a kind of mental strength I hadn't been able to harness in years. In connecting with myself, I was able to see what I'd been denying: my entrepreneurial spirit. Every breath became an opportunity to start fresh.

So, I battled all the judgments I had been putting on myself. Judgments of not being good enough. Of being a failure. I realized all of those thoughts hadn't been helping me. They were holding me back. I had been holding myself to others' standards and comparing my life and my situation to other people. In doing so, I had become the enemy. That was, until I decided to be brave enough to say no more. *I am enough.*

During this period of my life, what I view now as a terrifying and wonderful transition, I gave myself permission for the first time to celebrate all that I was, rather than get stuck on everything I wasn't. I focused not on regret or what I could've have done to change what happened, but instead I sought out clarity and self-trust. I began to believe in myself.

That belief manifested into something greater than I ever could have imagined. Something people spend lifetimes searching for and never find: *purpose*. I discovered my own purpose in helping people walk down the frightening and sometimes lonely road of self-discovery. For it is only once you know yourself and, more importantly, trust yourself that your goals can begin to transform from dreams into reality. It is not about what you "should be." It's about who you are now and all the incredible things you can accomplish, when you realize all you have to offer the world. Be willing to claim your power.

My purpose, I found, was to help others connect or reconnect to their purpose while growing their business. To give the wisdom and guidance necessary for women to find peace and clarity so they could grow into the fabulous, self-aware, and successful individuals they were always meant to be. It is only in the darkest of times that our light is able to shine the brightest. I am now living, breathing proof that it is more than possible for anyone and everyone to live a life of purpose, peace, and prosperity.

Today, as a Certified Professional Success Coach, I use my three decades of business experience in the corporate world and as an accomplished entrepreneur combined with the powerful mindset I found on my yoga mat to help women step into their power.

Don't get me wrong: I am in some ways still a Type-A, get-it-done girl. However, I have lost the "nothing is ever good enough" attitude and found strategies to end the constant judgment and inner conflict. After tearing some walls down and finding my true self on my yoga mat, I have discovered true success in owning the present moment.

Now I love teaching female entrepreneurs how to gain clarity and align their core values, beliefs, and goals to create the action plans needed for their own achievements. This allows them to live a life of success on their terms, rather than be defined by what someone else thinks they should be doing.

I use my no-victims-allowed sensibility to help my clients take their power back and own their truth and victories, while outlining their own rules and version of what success means to them.

If you are feeling overwhelmed, stressed, and like you have lost your power, and it's showing up in your business and personal life, please download this. I want to share with you the exact five things I did to gain clarity, connect to my core values, and take my power back. Please grab your free gift, *5 Steps to Take Your Power Back for Success* PDF here:

Email JenRyanTheAuthor@gmail.com

You can learn more about Jen Ryan at her website: www.jenryancoaching.com

ABOUT JEN RYAN: *Jen is an Amazon International best-selling author and a Certified Professional Success Coach with three decades of business experience in the corporate world and as an accomplished entrepreneur.*

Jen first teaches female entrepreneurs how to gain clarity so they can align their core values, beliefs, and goals. Then, the strategies and action plans needed for success can truly come to fruition.

She is known for her "no victims allowed" attitude, which helps her clients take their power back and own their truth and victories while defining their own rules and version of success. This comes from finding herself on her yoga mat days after her own world was turned upside down.

Jen realized she had to meet herself where she was, in that moment, because her Type-A, "get it done and nothing is ever good enough" attitude left her in constant state of self-judgment and inner conflict. This ultimately led her to actually give her power away. It was only when she was forced with the decision to face it or succumb to the defeat that she chose to take her power back.

From Homeless to Corporate

ROSITA SZATKOWSKA

IT WAS ONE OF the coldest nights I can remember in Northern California. I was sixteen at the time, homeless, drug-addicted, and very lost in life. I woke up on the floor of a dirty elevator at a train station. My best friend, Mike, was right next to me. He was my best friend and also the guy I did drugs with. We pulled ourselves up and started walking the streets, wondering where we would get our next fix. The only thing on my mind was how I would get high next. I did not care about where I would sleep next, what I would eat next, or if I would even be alive in the next few days.

My parents had changed the door locks on me the year prior. I had lost all my real friends and did not care about anything in life except getting high. That is how the next two years looked for me, until the month of my eighteenth birthday. That month, I had an awakening. Something came across my mind that led me to ask myself many questions about my life:

Is this it?

Will I be stuck forever?

Will I always be a kid on the streets?

I this what my life is worth?

In that same breath, I decided I would make something of myself. I realized I am beautiful, smart, and *worth it*! I have value and can do anything I put my mind to!

Of course, it is easier said than done. The first thing I did was stop using drugs and seek shelter. I was able to live with a friend and her mom in a small studio. I got a job and started to work extremely hard at it. I showed up on time every day and kept a positive attitude. I was so thankful I was finally able to make my own money and that I had a bed to sleep in. I stopped hanging out on the streets, and, most of all, I started to be honest with myself and everyone around me. I was on a mission to repair every single relationship I'd broken, due to my lies and drug use.

By the age of twenty, I was working two jobs and renting a super-cheap room. I had created really good, healthy routines for myself. I prayed to the higher power every day, worked hard, and stayed out of trouble.

Most important of all, I began telling myself positive things every day. This was how I kept my mind healthy. I told myself how great I was, how smart I was, and I would constantly envision what I wanted next in life. I would actually make myself believe that I already had what I wanted in life, even though this was long before I ever learned about the law of attraction.

By the time I was twenty-one, I had obtained an entry-level position with a grocery chain that was part of a Fortune 500 company. Within a few months, I had earned my first promotion to department manager. I would stay at work as long as I could, because I did not want to go home and face the drug use that was still surrounding me. Instead, after work, I read articles about leadership, courage, and integrity.

The store manager became my mentor and taught me how to be relentless in my pursuits. She also taught me that my past did not define me. She taught me about not limiting beliefs, and she signed me up for a self-help program. That program helped me gain clarity on my life and allowed me to start creating the life of my dreams. During the next eight years, I obtained six promotions within the company. I went from being one of the youngest store directors, operating multi-million-dollar operations with over 150 employees, to working in corporate and overseeing customer service and front-end operations in over three dozen stores.

By age twenty-eight, I already owned my third Mercedes, was engaged with my beautiful fiancée, had the cutest puppies, and was living the good life. My family had also begun communicating with me again, and I had earned back their trust. I am very proud to say I had also become an excellent role model for my younger siblings. I was someone they could look up to. However, one thing I would not stop doing was always envisioning what was next for me in life. I became addicted to my goals and continued to seek out what was possible for me to accomplish next. As soon as I got one promotion at work, I would already start envisioning the next role I wanted.

My story really does sound great on paper, right? The truth is it takes work, hard work, every day to be successful and really content with life as it is in the moment. It takes work to repair broken-down relationships and have a lot of "clean up" conversations that no one likes having.

I had to learn how to be brave and work through all the fears we, as human beings, face on a daily basis. I had to learn to be self-assured and stop constantly comparing myself to the rest of the world. I am gay, I have short hair, I have tattoos, I am from Poland, and I have a past, but don't we all? I have learned throughout these ten years that the past is just that... a past. Life is now!

I realized we all need to gain clarity, set goals, and take action with a positive attitude every day. This way, one day at a time, we can all create our envisioned lives. As a millennial, I know it is not easy to live in this society, where we are inundated with social media. I don't question at all why other millennials don't know what to do next or why they have anxiety about their futures. Even with all my success, I have often had these same feelings.

A year ago, when I was a store director at the Fortune 500 company, I resigned and went to another company, because, in my mind, I did not think I had a happy future with that company. I felt as though I wasn't enough. I ended up returning to the company four months later, but it was super-important for me to leave. Leaving the company was part of finding my way and finding myself.

I believe we need to give ourselves permission to grow and be okay with making a change and making decisions. As millennials know nowadays, there are so many expectations, but what is the payoff? You need to ask yourself, "Are you really happy" and "What is unhappiness costing you?"

That is what inspired me to start my own Success Coaching business for millennials. I completely understand 100% of what millennials are going through in this century. I am successful and happy, but I know what it took for me to get here. I know what steps you have to take, what you have to do daily, weekly, monthly, and consistently, to really live an authentic and transformed life in this world.

That is why I created the Millennial Life Mastery Signature Program. It is a twelve-week mastermind program that includes weekly live video sessions with me, weekly workbook assignments that build on top of one another, and bi-weekly mastermind video calls with people who are in the same boat as you. In this program, you learn how to gain clarity, improve your self-esteem, set actual goals for your life, and take real action to help achieve those goals. Also, week by week, you get fun homework that helps you learn to use the tools you need to make it in the world as a millennial.

I am a true example that anything is possible in life. It doesn't matter how defeated you feel right now, how lost you are, with an aching soul, or unsure where to turn next. I am here to tell you that you can get out of it and really be happy and confident, living a life you truly love without constant comparison.

Remember: life is right now. Wasting time worrying about tomorrow just takes away from your real true dream life. I went from being homeless to corporate to public speaker to Success Coach and on to best-selling author, all within ten years. I have learned all the tools you need, and now it is my mission to share those tools with you.

I want to teach you and guide you, so you can be your best version of yourself every day. I want you to start living your life and achieving whatever your heart desires. I sincerely want to thank you for taking the time to read my story, and I would also love to hear about yours.

I am opening up my calendar for the next few days and offering a free eleven-minute Success Call just for you, because you're reading this book and I know you are serious about taking action and making a difference in your life.

Click on the link below right now to schedule your success call with me. I can't wait to chat with you!

https://rositaszatkowska.as.me/SuccessCall

But that's not all! I still have one more free gift for you, to help you on your journey of living a powerful and confident, comparison-free life. Just send an e-mail to me at RositaMillennialCoach@gmail.com containing the words, "YES, I Want My Free Gift," and it is all yours!

By the way, that store manager who took me under her wing and promoted me in my first role... I call her my mom now. She coached me, mentored me, and guided me all these years. So, remember: whatever you want to do in life, you cannot do it alone. It is okay to get help, to seek coaching and advice. It helps you to be stronger and much better! At the end of the day, sometimes it is better to learn from someone else's mistakes!

With love,

> Rosita S.
> Success Coach for Millennials

P.S. I am teaching a FREE Masterclass on The 5 Steps To Go From Constantly Comparing Yourself to Complete Confidence So You Can Achieve Your Goals and Enjoy Total Fulfillment in Your Life!

Register Here Now: www.rositaszatkowska.com/masterclass

I am so excited for you to join and can't wait to chat with you!!

###

ABOUT ROSITA SZATKOWSKA: *Rosita is a certified coach and speaker, who works with millennials by helping them achieve their* goals and desired success. She also encourages women to live courageously, confidently, and without constant comparison. In her teens, Rosita found herself homeless and addicted to drugs. She realized there was more to life and her past experiences did not define her. Armed with her positive mindset, confidence, courage, and a strong work ethic, Rosita was hired into an entry-level position within a Fortune 500 company. She quickly rose to become one of the youngest store directors in the company. After successfully managing multi-million-dollar store operations, she obtained a position in corporate management.

Rosita found a greater purpose in helping others succeed. She inspires them to get "un-stuck" and gain self-confidence. This enables them to live the life they desire, regardless of background or circumstances. She holds her clients accountable for themselves and discourages hiding behind facades. Rosita is a true optimist, leader, millennial, and entrepreneur. She considers it her mission in life to inspire other lives she touches to "go for it" and live their life now, enabling her clients to create their life dreams one day at a time.

We Are All the Cosmic Dancer

SALLY LAKSHMI THURLEY

IT HIT ME ONE AFTERNOON, in the old, dark study hall at boarding school, when I was sixteen: something had changed. It was like a switch had been flicked. In that moment, I left everything I knew about living in the world behind. I didn't want it. If that was what made people so angry, so miserable, then I didn't want it. If the only way I could get admiration, to be like them, then I rejected it. I lived between worlds at this stage, trying to follow the wisdom of my awakening as a kid and working out how to live creatively in the world without selling my soul. I also had checked out on myself, given up.

I had full blown PTSD but didn't know it, permanently in fight-or-flight mode and living at school, because living at home was not a safe option. Not only was I lost and stressed, but I was living with chronic illness; I spent my time between my dormitory, the boarding school house nurse, and hospital.

I had a lot of spirit, however, and found, if I lived flat out, milking every moment, I could deal with the pain. This became an effective mechanism for me and I made sure to experience as much of life as I could, which meant I partied hard to relieve the tension. To make things more complex, I went and married at the tender age of twenty-one, to try and create the safe and happy family life I missed.

The call of spirit was very strong. The world is a harsh place for a mystical kid. The call was always so strong that I never felt it as separate from life. The more I explored and followed the call, the more intense life seemed to come, and it didn't help that I was running in overdrive all the time. The search for wisdom, for truth, since the age of eleven led me to meeting an enlightened teacher at twenty-five. Once I heard him speak in a meditation course, I knew that was it. I was home. Whatever he had, I wanted, and I was meant to have. I stayed and worked and studied for the next twenty years there, throwing myself into the path of self-realization. Life didn't ease up. In fact, it got harder.

When I was on partner number two after my divorce, and after the death of my mother and finally leaving my family dynamic, I began to question my reason for being. How come I could be so connected and have all this wonderful spiritual life and still life seemed to suck? Like, harder than for those around me?

I started seeing my life as a divine experiment. Wanting answers wasn't enough, by this stage. I wanted a bloody miracle. I was in a relationship with someone I finally really loved, who was a challenge in every way and pushed my nervous system over the edge. I had an adrenal breakdown and then saw how this relationship was heading for the rocks. It was time to stop the shipwrecks.

Something inside of me made a pact that I was meant to work something out. It came from a determination to be the best version of me, whatever that looked like, although it had to resonate with what I felt deep inside—loving, wise. I didn't have to be a nice person. I didn't even care if I died. But I wanted to crack the human code, enlightenment—whatever was available to me, and be *that*, with no care about how it was received or judged by the world.

I took on becoming a non-judgmental witness and integrating good spiritual philosophy with life. I walked into a fire; the universe met me and figuratively pushed me over a cliff. I lost everything: the use of my legs, my partner, my home, my community. The ultimate free fall. I'd done the biggest apprenticeship of all time, and now it was time to be what I'd become. I was to live the dharma and had been given a fresh start. I knew what was healing, I knew who I was, I knew God. All doubt had been removed, and the healing was in walking off into the sunset with nothing, knowing I had full faith and support by the Divine working through me.

The PTSD was finally diagnosed during this the mother of all wipeouts. When you pray hard enough, when you make a deal with the Divine, you will get all you want and must be prepared for how it will come. My reason for being was answered. Once I got it, I didn't miss a moment to launch a business, take all I had learned to the world, and become the spiritual teacher life had qualified me to be. I understood love was my way to move from being overly active and tightly wired to being graceful, slow, and peaceful. I'm still getting accustomed to that.

I'm here to challenge the status quo and create a new way, a new spiritual model that includes spiritual entrepreneurship while working toward world peace and healing my way. When we start to observe life and not get sucked into thinking it is happening to us (certainly not for any sinister reason), then the fruits always come. I finally listened to and accepted the message that I am meant to be independent and learn not to depend or need anyone or anything but spirit. In choosing to allow my relationship to do what it needed to do and contemplate why we suffer, I downloaded how grace works and how to get through with peace and love. It worked.

There are many great yogic principles that are thousands of years old and as relevant now as back then. Only the need for a new perspective creates new expressions of what has always been eternally known and will never change. Many had a huge impact on me, but when it came to dharma and working out what I am here to do, I contemplated *Sahaja Samadhi*.

We are all supremely free—*As we Are*. Not as something or somebody else. You are who you *are*: whether you are happy, contemplative, passionate, internal, grumpy, joyful, negative, or positive, you are free. The deal is we just don't know it. But someone who's established in their self is free. Nothing needs to change but our awareness and experience of this.

This led to my coming up with the distinction about wants and desires. We suffer because we identify too much with the body and with the mind. This is ignorance. The truth is we are not that. We suffer because we push away what is so, in the present moment. Or, like I used to do, we gorge on life in an endless need to suppress the pain. The ego wants the perfect partner, the best qualification, fame, money, cars, houses—everything to be perfect. The soul doesn't give a shit. It just is. Pure bliss. So, to overcome suffering and move forward on a soul level, we need to align the human want with the soul want, what we already are. I created an entire model and mentoring process around this, which is the basis of my book.

Working spiritualty is about moving from the gross to the subtle, from the mundane to the divine. Whatever we think we want, we need to find the truth of it, what we *really* want. Then, hold that as the biggest spiritual practice of our life. It will give *all* the solutions, the answers, the action steps. If you think you want money, look closer at why, go inward. Sure, there are the reasons, like paying the bills, moving to a better home for your kids, and so forth, but the real reason will be quite different. Discover what that is, and then there is the answer on how to really get what you want, which most likely has adapted from the process.

I call this my Spanda Method. Spanda is the Sanskrit word for vibration. We all come from Divine will and have that running through us. My method uses language that follows the movement of consciousness; it uses what we most want as the way home. When we remember home, we find peace. Peace is the anchor of life.

Be like a monk in the world and align with your God-given purpose. This is the path of the She-Monk. Use your life as your spiritual practice: know your spiritual personality, and use it to create with the freedom of who you really are. I celebrate all that has happened and, at times, still happens. The journey of the body isn't the real story. It's when we know we are so much more and not limited by what happens to us. Life is bloody wonderful!

I'd love you to know what it is you most want. If you're the kind of person who wants to embody their essence, then I have something for you. Are you someone who wants the liberation of knowing you are peace, love, and freedom at all times in life, no matter what and want to contribute to an enlightened society in the way of spiritual leadership? Then please send me your email to sallyshemonk@gmail.com, and I will send you my signature meditation, to discover your soul's want

It will help you:

- ❖ Know what to do in any and all situations, in alignment with spirit.
- ❖ Free your busy mind to clarity.
- ❖ Spiritually expand from within to become an awakened leader.

I invite you to discover your spiritual personality and learn more of the She-Monk work:

http://discover.spiritualpersonalityquiz.com/

http://bit.ly/SheMonk

www.sallythurley.com

###

ABOUT SALLY LAKSHMI THURLEY: *Sally is a published author of the book,* She-Monk: Daily Life is the New Spiritual Practice. *She is a spiritual teacher, artist, and entrepreneur driven to create an enlightened society and world peace. She takes people into their inner worlds to find their essence, their reason for being, and then brand that as their soul-ignited brand. After spending decades studying and living spiritual practice and philosophy with an ashram, Sally has learned how to merge spiritual practice, self-awareness, personal development, and service to humanity through an entrepreneurial venture as a soul brand. She also has her own spiritual learning center, the Self-Knowledge Sangha.*

www.sallythurley.com

###

FIND THE AUTHORS

Discover more about the powerful and inspirational authors featured *in Mastering Your Inner Game*:

Jenn Scalia	http://jennscalia.com
AJ Mihrzad	http://onlinesupercoach.com/start
Jono Petrohilos	http://facebook.com/jono/petrohilos
Cat Almanzor	catalmanzorSheHeals@gmail.com
Mary Allison Brown	www.maryallisonbrown.com
Vitale Buford	www.vitalebuford.com
Shawn Henson	www.ShawnHenson.com
Susanna Esther Kashiemer	www.susannaesther.com
Sara Kirsch	www.marketingisnotselling.com
Christy Little	www.thedancingoptimist.com
Roseanney Liu	www.roseanney.com
Jen Ryan	www.jenryancoaching.com
Rosita Szatkowska	rositaMillennialCoach@gmail.com
Sally Thurley	www.sallythurley.com

Made in the USA
Middletown, DE
10 October 2018